Two Views of Life

Secular Humanism
and
Radical Fundamentalism

☆☆☆☆☆☆

Brian Bolton

m & m Press
Fayetteville, Arkansas

TWO VIEWS OF LIFE

Printed in the United States of America.

First Edition published 1988

ISBN 0-943099-01-3

Contents

Part III—Fundamentalism and Death

Part IV—Fundamentalism and Sports

DEDICATION

Rev. Joseph Gabriel Bane died on November 14, 1986 at the age of 86 in Orangevale, Florida. The youngest of eight children, he was born into impoverished circumstances in rural Tennessee. By virtue of hard work, Joseph attained a good education and became Jesus' faithful servant.

Rev. Bane received degrees in philosophy and theology from the Southeastern Evangelical Seminary and was ordained in the Gospel Free Will denomination. He held positions ranging from country preacher to distinguished professor of moral science at Southeastern during his long career. After retiring in 1982, he lived with his daughter in Fayetteville, Arkansas, before moving to Florida in May, 1986.

Rev. Bane dedicated his life to spreading the Good News of Jesus' ethical commandments to all people. He was an exemplary Christian, always concerned about others, tolerant of all religious views, forgiving of the most serious transgressions, displaying compassion for all life forms, and he was absolutely non-materialistic. In fact, he never owned a home or automobile and gave his entire salary to charity.

Unpopular with religious fundamentalists, J. G. Bane dismissed the dogma of biblical literalism as nonsensical, advocated Christian support and love as the solution to abortion, considered the battle against cigarette smoking to be a moral issue, and

Two Views of Life

believed Buddha, Confucius, Zoroaster, and Mohammed to be prophets of the same rank as Jesus.

Rev. Bane was a tireless advocate of strict gun control laws, regarded hunting as a morally indefensible tradition, argued that Darwinian evolution does not contradict true Christian faith, strongly opposed capital punishment, and regarded Martin Luther King, Jr. as the greatest American hero.

In view of his abhorrence of religious zealotry and his lifelong commitment to social justice, Rev. Bane's friends and family were not surprised when he announced shortly before his death that he was a secular humanist. He was also a Christian in the only meaningful sense of the term.

Rev. Dr. Edgar V. Bradwell

PREFACE

Due to the untiring efforts of fundamentalist preachers and Religious Right political activists, secular humanism has emerged from philosophical obscurity to become a household obscenity within the short span of 15 years. Few Americans have not heard or read something about this godless, communist-sponsored conspiracy to infiltrate the public schools, destroy the traditional family, and overthrow the U.S. government. Yet, even in 1987, there are fewer than 100,000 card-carrying secular humanists in the U.S.!

What were the main events that accounted for the meteoric rise in popular acquaintance with secular humanism? The initial impetus was the publication of *Humanist Manifesto II* in 1973, a brief statement of secular humanistic principles that provided an ideal target for the hatemongers of the New Religious Right. The earliest formal attacks on secular humanism were The Heritage Foundation's *Secular Humanism and the Schools: The Issue Whose Time Has Come* (197?) and Rev. Homer Duncan's *Secular Humanism: The Most Dangerous Religion in America* (1979).

The most successful expression of hatred toward secular humanists, by far, was Rev. Tim LaHaye's *The Battle for the Mind* (1980), which sold almost a half million copies. Rev. LaHaye's venomous remarks are quoted extensively in the first two chapters in this volume. Still, it is safe to say that no in-

Two Views of Life

dividual has more consistently insinuated that secular humanists are Satan's agents than the inimitable Rev. Jerry Falwell, radical fundamentalist extraordinairé and founder of the doubly misnamed "Moral Majority."

Two quotes illustrate the good Rev. Falwell's unchristian attitude toward his despised enemy:

> . . .we see the promotion of a secular humanistic philosophy throughout our educational system. This view of mankind has no biblical basis. . .this humanistic philosophy is permeating our society. . . . The end result has been the breakdown of the family, a 40% divorce rate, moral permissiveness, a drug epidemic, and an anti-American, anti-free enterprise philosophy among our youth (*America's 6 Deadly Sins*, no date).

* * *

> The question is. . .whose morality will be legislated. Will it be the moral relativism of humanism, resulting as it does in hedonism, abortion, infanticide, suicide, euthanasia, and general chaos? Or will it be the morality of the Judeo-Christian culture? (*Fundamentalist Journal*, July/August, 1985).

Preface

It is important to make a clear distinction between the Revs. Jerry Falwell, Tim LaHaye, Jimmy Swaggart, and other radical fundamentalist preachers and their followers, on the one hand, and the vast majority of Christian fundamentalists in America who reject the political extremism of the Religious Right, on the other. Radical fundamentalists, who are also known as authoritarian fundamentalists and fascist fundamentalists, want to inflict their narrow religious dogma on everybody else. For example, they promote mandatory prayer in the public schools, they demand that "scientific creationism" be taught as an alternative to Darwinian evolution, and they advocate a constitutional amendment to outlaw abortion.

Although there is no standard definition of radical fundamentalism currently available, the characterization adopted by Fundamentalists Anonymous, a support group for former fundamentalists, is helpful. They define fundamentalism as a mindset rather than a set of doctrines: "The fundamentalist mindset is authoritarian, intolerant, and compulsive about imposing itself on others." This brief formulation was expanded by John Windsor of Little Rock, a self-proclaimed (nonradical) fundamentalist, in a manner that viewers of the televangelists can appreciate:

> . . . it is a stunted and warped form of the historical Evangelical faith. . . rather than concentrating on the central theme of God the Savior of sinners, it spends all its time condemning such

things as drinking, dancing, makeup, and discussing the Rapture, Russia and Israel, the common Market, 666, and the 7-headed, 10-horned beast of Revelation.

Beginning in the late 1970's, secular humanists were fully occupied in answering the continuous attacks by far-right religious fanatics. But by the middle 1980's secular humanists had moved to the offense against the real threat to freedom in America. Full credit should be given to civil liberties watchdog groups like Americans United for Separation of Church and State and People for the American Way, which have put the radical fundamentalists on the defense. Mainline religious organizations have also responded to the Religious Right's propaganda. A good example is the monograph, *Secular Humanism and the Public Schools* (1986), published by the National Council of Churches of Christ in the U.S.A.

If it is not already obvious, the author's position in this monumental battle between Good and Evil will now be stated unequivocally: I am a secular humanist. The 19 chapters comprising this volume, all of which were published previously, present one individual's attempt to expose radical fundamentalists for the bullies, hypocrites, and know-nothings that they are. It is important to emphasize that my quarrel is not with the vast majority of Christian fundamentalists but only with the small minority of fundamentalist zealots who have no respect for the rights and beliefs of other Americans.

Most of the chapters have been updated for this book, and some have been revised or expanded. Some titles have been modified. The original publication sources are acknowledged in the Credits section. The chapter on Christian Humanism in the first section is an edited compilation of published letters by J. G. Bane, to whom the volume is dedicated. All royalties that accrue from sales of the book will be donated to the Arkansas Affiliate of the American Civil Liberties Union, an organization committed to the preservation of religious freedom in the U.S.

Brian Bolton
August, 1987

Part I

Secular Humanism

Introduction

Although tens of millions of Americans are acquainted with the radical fundamentalists' favorite epithet, few people can identify or describe a secular humanist. In a speech to the National Conference of Christians and Jews, former vice president Walter Mondale, who is a Christian, said that during the 1984 presidential campaign he was attacked as "an atheist and secular humanist, whatever that is." Interestingly, his older brother, Rev. Lester Mondale, was a signer of *Humanist Manifesto I* in 1933.

Secular humanism is a philosophical position that maintains that moral principles are derived through human reasoning, rather than being god-given. Commenting on this postulate, Rev. H. D. McCarty stated, "This is the devil's masterpiece . . . man's belief in himself — man finding God unnecessary — man making it on his own. This is the way of total destruction." Gladys Cole of Fayetteville was even more direct: ". . . Godless humanists are . . . anti-American, anti-God, and promote population control by abortion, euthanasia, infanticide, and suicide. . ."

Because of the avalanche of publicity accorded by radical fundamentalists, individuals of every political and religious persuasion have freely invoked the specter of secular humanism. For example, Rev. Thom Robb of Harrison, Arkansas, who is the national chaplain of the Knights of the Ku Klux Klan, charged that the U.S. government supports "policies of homosexuality, race mixing, secular humanism, abortion, and Zionism." William Gleaton of Albany, Georgia was fired from his job at a Firestone Tire plant because he refused to conduct a corporate training program that he said "constituted a form of secular humanism." He sued and reached an out-of-court settlement with Firestone!

Secular humanism has also provided an attractive target for humorists, comedians and jokesters. Ridiculing fundamentalists in the Greenville, Tennessee textbook trial, syndicated columnist Mike Royko said that he was sure that fundamentalists would agree with him "that the presence of women on a golf course—a traditional male haven—is another evil example of secular humanism." Spoofing the Mobile, Alabama secular humanism trial, Ralph P. Forbes of Little Rock filed a lawsuit charging that the observance of Halloween in the public schools promotes the establishment of Satanism as the official state religion. Among the 14 defendants listed was "the High Priest of Secular Humanism."

Six chapters comprise part I. **What is Secular Humanism?** responds to some of the more outrageous allegations by radical fundamentalists about secular humanism. A brief historical overview along with capsule summaries of secular humanist

positions on four controversial issues is given in
Secular Humanist Philosophy. Ten basic propositions of secular humanism are presented in **Tenets
of Secular Humanism**. Ten moral principles derived from the Gospel are succinctly stated in **Jesus'
Ten Commandments**. In **Jesus and Secular Humanism** documentation is provided for the argument that secular humanist philosophy is consistent with Jesus' primary ethical teachings. Finally,
Christian Humanism outlines general positions on
moral and social issues that are held by the largest
segment of the humanist population, Christian
humanists.

Chapter 1

What is Secular Humanism?

In August, 1985 Fayetteville physician Dr. Doty Murphy was interviewed concerning his decision to educate his children at home. His explanation was essentially that there was too much "humanism" in the public schools. It is difficult to understand how a presumably well-educated individual could be so ignorant about one of the major philosophical and literary movements of Western civilization. Yet, Dr. Murphy's view is not unusual among Christian fundamentalists. Where did this negative conception of humanism originate and what function does it serve in the fundamentalist mentality?

During the past 10 years almost every societal problem in the U.S. has been attributed at one time or another by fundamentalists to humanism. These include drugs, pornography, abortion, divorce, teenage pregnancy, homosexuality, political corruption, educational decline, genital herpes, AIDS, and just about everything else. More generally, the humanistic conspiracy is charged with corrupting the entire moral foundation of America. Reasonable people naturally ask, What is this menace called humanism? What are its historical roots? What are its basic tenets? And, perhaps most importantly, Who are the humanists?

One useful approach to the subject is to examine the critics' conception of humanism. The following statements are taken almost verbatim from the *Battle for the Mind* (1980). Written by Rev. Tim LaHaye, who holds a Doctor of Ministries degree from Western Conservative Baptist Seminary, this volume has been a popular source book for preachers and laypersons of fundamentalist persuasion.

• • •Humanism is the most dangerous religion in the world today.

• • •Most of the evils in the world today can be traced to humanism.

• • •Humanists are the mortal enemy of all pro-moral Americans, and the most serious threat to our nation in its entire history.

• • •Humanists endorse equal rights, homosexuality, abortion, marijuana, disarmament, and everything else that is harmful to America.

• • •Almost every sexual law that is required to maintain a morally sane society has been struck down by the humanists, so that man may follow his animal appetites.

• • •Humanists hope to name their own dictator who will create a humanist utopia—an atheistic, socialistic, amoral society for America.

• • •No humanist is qualified to hold any government office in America.

This brief summary constitutes a rather strongly worded indictment of something labelled generically as "humanism." No wonder Dr. Murphy decided to educate his children at home, considering Rev. LaHaye's revelations about the humanistic infiltration of the schools:

• • •Humanism has developed a stranglehold on American public education.

• • •The increased breakdown of the home, alcoholism, suicide, homosexuality, and drug addiction can be attributed to humanist educators.

• • •It is probable that a large percentage of all atheists in America are employed in education, where they have access to the minds of young people.

• • •This country's leading humanistic educators, lawmakers, and judges are committed to doing away with every vestige of the responsible, moral behavior that distinguished man from animals.

• • •John Dewey and his disciples have taken over the public schools and turned them into tax-supported religious shrines that waste the potential of our young.

• • •The chaos in today's public education system is in direct proportion to its religious obsession with humanism.

Most readers will be asking themselves at this point, How can anybody take these charges seriously? Obviously, no reasonable individual would put any stock in such outlandish, extreme, and bizarre allegations. But a small minority of Christians have heard Jerry Falwell, Jimmy Swaggart, James Robison, and their local fundamentalist ministers repeat these charges on numerous occasions, leading them to accept the allegations as true. In his call for spiritual and moral revival in America, outlined in *Listen, America!* (1980), Jerry Falwell listed the five major national sins: abortion, homosexuality, pornography, humanism, and the fractured family. This is certainly one source of impetus for the growing Christian school movement.

To comprehend the genesis of this wild thinking, which is simply unmitigated religious zealotry, it is necessary to begin at the beginning. First, what is it that Rev. LaHaye is referring to when he speaks of humanism? He defines humanism as man's attempt to solve his problems independently of God. In fact, this is a reasonably accurate definition of one variety of humanism, called secular humanism. Specifically, *secularism* refers to a system of doctrines and practices that rejects any form of religious faith and worship, while *humanism* is a philosophical perspective that emphasizes human interests, values, and activities.

It is clear then that secular humanism is a nontheistic humanism. But there are other forms of nontheistic humanism, such as that practiced by the Fellowship of Religious Humanists and the Ethical Culture Societies. Among the theistic humanists, the best known doctrinal groups are probably Unitarianism, humanistic Judaism, and Christian humanism. In light of Rev. LaHaye's scathing characterization of humanism, the latter group may strike some readers as a blatant contradiction in terms, even an impossibility! How can God-fearing, Bible-believing Christians possibly be affiliated with an atheistic, amoral, socialistic philosophy that is destroying America?

It will surprise most fundamentalists to learn that the intellectual and cultural movement called humanism that initiated the Renaissance in Europe in the fourteenth century was not necessarily unreligious or anti-religious. In fact, most of the leading humanist figures, including Erasmus and Thomas More, were devout Christians. The roots of Christian humanism are found in both Greco-Roman antiquity and in the Judaic-Christian heritage. Readers interested in exploring the origins, character, and goals of an "authentic Christian humanism" are referred to the short volume, *Secular Humanism: Threat and Challenge* (1982) by Robert Webber, a professor of theology at Wheaton College.

Secular Humanism

Despite its title, Professor Webber's carefully argued presentation is less an attack on secular humanism than it is a doctrinal formulation of Christian humanism. Professor Webber is appropriately critical of Religious Right extremists generally, and the so-called Moral Majority in particular. For example, he describes the Religious Right's support of militarism to protect "God's interests" as a blaspheming against God's church and cites favorably Bishop Matthiesen of Amarillo, Texas who encouraged Christians to quit their jobs assembling nuclear bombs.

Professor Webber repeatedly reminds the Moral Majority that America is not a Christian nation, but a pluralistic society, and condemns Falwellian religious nationalism as a perversion of the Gospel of Jesus Christ. However, Professor Webber also views secular humanism as a threat to society (because it has no ultimate basis for morality, he says), and is "one of many bold attempts of the doomed powers of evil to regain a footing in the world."

For the most part, Rev. LaHaye and the fundamentalists are really attacking only secular humanists and similar groups, rather than all humanists. What is it about the secular humanists that attracts the animosity of fundamentalists and moderate evangelical Christians as well? Even the diplomat of evangelical preachers, Billy Graham, recently decried the "secular critics who have invented a creed which is the worship of humanity." Although there are obviously numerous points of difference

9

between secular humanists and their enemies, there is one central Christian postulate that underlies all other differences.

Professor Webber diagnoses the major flaw in secular humanist philosophy to be its failure to take into account the evil inherent in human nature. In contrast, Christian humanism is predicated on the fallen moral nature of man, *i.e.*, humans are by nature sinful creatures. Rev. LaHaye says much the same thing when he states that because human nature is fallen, sinful, and untrustworthy, a civilized culture must have moral laws based on biblical absolutes. Secular humanists believe that human beings have the innate capacity for goodness and decency, and that human goodness will emerge if society encourages and nurtures virtuous behavior. Furthermore, secular humanists maintain that human values are derived through a rational intellectual process rather than received through divine revelation.

Ironically, it is difficult to dispute the fundamentalist contention that humans are by natural inclination sinful, evil, and untrustworthy, in light of the great religiously inspired atrocities of Western history, *e.g.*, the Crusades, the Inquisitions, numerous Holy Wars, and the Salem Witchcraft Trials. And in current times we witness the barbaric killing in Northern Ireland, the Middle East, and many other locations. Prominent examples in Arkansas include the reprehensible activities of the Covenant, Sword, and Arm of the Lord and the neo-Nazi religious organization called The Order.

It is easy to understand why Rev. LaHaye concluded that "history proves that unrestrained man has a natural penchant for criminality and inhumanity towards his fellowman"!

While this historical and anecdotal evidence certainly weighs heavily in favor of the fundamentalist argument for "fallen" human nature, it obviously contradicts the proposition that biblically-derived moral absolutes mitigate against human misbehavior. It must be admitted, however, that the issue of moral absolutism *vs.* moral relativism would be virtually impossible to resolve by appeal to empirical evidence. Regardless, the purpose here is not to argue the issue, but only to identify it as central to understanding the irrational reaction of fundamentalists to the philosophy of secular humanism.

The fundamentalists' attacks on secular humanism have continued unabated. For example, a summary in *The Voice of Freedom*, an ultra-conservative, fundamentalist magazine, stated that humanists "believe" in abortion, euthanasia, suicide, divorce, homosexuality, fornication, adultery, and pornography. In a two-part television sermon titled "The New Evangelists," Rev. Jimmy Swaggart repeated many of the standard charges.

For example, Rev. Swaggart identified three primary marketing vehicles of secular humanism: *Playboy*, *Penthouse*, and *Hustler* for young and middle-aged men; afternoon soap operas for housewives; and Saturday morning cartoon programs for children. The values that are inculcated include, of course, homosexuality, adultery and illicit sex, alcohol abuse, and disrespect for biblical moral precepts. Rev. Swaggart concluded that the television industry, which he calls "the greatest force for evil ever offered into mankind's hand," is thoroughly dominated by secular humanists.

Postscript. On February 21, 1988 Rev. Swaggart publicly confessed to unspecified sins committed with a prostitute in New Orleans. He was subsequently defrocked by the Assemblies of God after he refused to accept a one year preaching ban ordered by the Executive Presbytery of the church.

Chapter 2

Secular Humanist Philosophy

Humanism refers to the literary and philosophical movement that emerged in fourteenth century Europe, signaling a shift from the theological studies of the Middle Ages to a concern with secular learning and contemporary life. Humanist scholars studied the classical Greek and Roman ideas and formulations about law, politics, and philosophy as a basis for addressing basic moral and ethical questions.

While there was no specific philosophical doctrine that characterized Humanism, the views of humanist scholars were almost invariably anti-traditional and anti-scholastic, and occasionally, anti-theological, but not necessarily irreligious and seldom anti-Christian. Ironically, in view of fundamentalist criticism, humanists condemned Scholastic philosophy while advocating a return to the original sources of Christian doctrine, the Bible and St. Augustine in particular.

Humanism represented a merging of the intellectual attitudes of classical antiquity with the reverential concerns of the Middle Ages. As a result, humanists rejected the absolute authority of the church, while stressing human rational capacity

13

and individual choice and responsibility. Even though humanists then and now reject ecclesiastical authority, it simply is not true that "The foundation stone of all humanistic thought is atheism," as Rev. LaHaye charges in *The Battle for The Mind*. Furthermore, it is equally preposterous to allege that "Humanistic principles contradict almost every basic concept of biblical revelation," as Rev. LaHaye does.

In fact, the largest segment of the humanist population in America by far consists of Christian humanists. Robert Webber in *Secular Humanism: Threat and Challenge* defines Christian humanism as a humanistic doctrine that emerges from the ethical and theological teachings of Jesus Christ. Basic to Christian humanism is the belief that God himself (in the person of Jesus) became human, experienced humanity, and cared about the human situation, thus justifying the earthly human concerns of Christians. The central values of Christian humanism are exemplified in Jesus Christ, *e.g.*, peace, love, compassion, kindness, humility, gentleness, and patience.

Secular humanists and Christian humanists agree almost completely on the human values promulgated in conjunction with Jesus' ethical teachings. Secular humanists and Christian humanists concur on the centrality of *humane* values, *e.g.*, compassion, concern, and forgiveness, and on commitment to *humanitarian* action, *i.e.*, dedication to promotion of human welfare, through elimination of suffering and enhancement of human happiness. Although secular humanists and Christian humanists disagree regarding the ultimate source of humane values and humanitarian commitment, there is no reason why this difference should preclude peaceful coexistence or even mutual cooperation, considering the substantial common ground that is shared by these two life orientations.

The secular values and attitudes of Renaissance humanism were amplified in the eighteenth century movement known as the Enlightenment or Age of Reason. Enlightenment thinkers, such as Hume, Voltaire, and Rousseau, stressed reliance on human rationality and scientific logic, empirical study of human nature through social analysis, rejection of theological authority and sacred writings, and especially, denial of the Christian dogma of original sin.

The latter point is probably the main reason why the usually restrained Rev. LaHaye concluded that the Enlightenment "produced some of the greatest philosophical evils in the history of mankind." It should be noted in fairness that the excessive and exclusive reliance on reason and the extreme anti-theological attitudes of major Enlightenment propagandists produced a concurrent counter-Enlightenment that Rev. LaHaye would most surely have joined.

Before proceeding to a discussion of various concrete issues, a brief recapitulation may be helpful. Secular humanism is synonymous with the ethical doctrine of humanitarianism which holds that human nature may be perfected without divine grace or intervention. This contrasts sharply with the Christian axiom that states that because human nature is fallen, "All naive hopes that individuals will change and society will become better are utopian and false." (according to Professor Webber). Secular humanists maintain that life is the preeminent human value, and reject all hypothesized supernatural causes and explanations. Secular humanism is a practical, everyday philosophy that has as its singular goal the enhancement of human earthly existence.

It should be apparent from this short summary that secular humanism cannot reasonably be classified as a religion, as numerous fundamentalist critics have done. For example, Rev. LaHaye calls (secular) humanism "a subtle form of religious evil" and concludes that it is "the most deceptive of all religious philosophies." The standard dictionary definition of religion is belief in a divine creator of the universe that is to be obeyed and worshipped. Clearly, secular humanism does not qualify as a religion using this definition.

On the other hand, if a much broader definition is adopted, i.e., religion is a system of beliefs and values that provide a framework for living, then secular humanism would qualify as a religion. But then so would every other quasi-philosophical system from skepticism to vegetarianism! The fundamentalists' ploy in insisting that secular humanism is a religion is to enable them to declare that teaching the "humanist doctrines of evolution, sex education, and values clarification" in the public schools is a violation of the principle of separation of church and state.

Rather than formally reviewing the central tenets of secular humanism, I am going to outline secular humanist positions regarding several issues that are crucial in fundamentalists' attacks. Readers interested in examining formal statements of secular humanist philosophy are referred to *Humanist Manifesto I & II* (1973) and to *A Secular Humanist Declaration* (1980) for succinct treatments, and to Corliss Lamont's *The Philosophy of Humanism* (1982) for a detailed presentation. The primary journals of secular humanism are *The Humanist*, *Free Inquiry*, and *The American Rationalist*.

Evolution

As every Arkansan surely knows, Christian fundamentalists argued unsuccessfully in federal court in 1982 that what they call "scientific creationism" should be taught in public school science courses as a legitimate alternative to Darwinian evolution. After patiently listening to the fundamentalists' arguments, Judge William Overton concluded that "creation science" is not science at all, but rather religious dogma translated into pseudo-scientific jargon. Despite this and other outright legal defeats, fundamentalists remain dedicated to their goal of foisting creationism on public school children. Why? There are two reasons: fundamentalists regard the Bible as "infallible and inerrant" as Jerry

Falwell asserts, and they simply don't understand modern scientific logic.

The origins of life on earth date back some 3 to 4 billion years and the sequential process of evolutionary development has been described in considerable detail. We know that humans evolved from more primitive ape-like animals during the last 10 million years or so, and we know further that humans share a common heritage with all life forms on the planet. All available evidence from scientific disciplines ranging from anthropology, archaeology, biochemistry, and comparative anatomy, through genetics to zoology supports one overwhelming *scientific fact*: all life on earth evolved from simpler forms.

A scientific theory is a cohesive explanation of observed phenomena that is based on empirical evidence and rational argument. Scientific facts are simply the best knowledge currently available; scientific facts are continually modified and supplanted by new knowledge. What fundamentalist critics fail to appreciate about the scientific method is that there are no ultimate truths in science. All scientific knowledge, whether labelled hypotheses, principles, laws, theories, or even "facts," consists of provisional statements that are subject to revision or replacement. The Darwinian theory of organic evolution can be reasonably regarded as a scientific fact because virtually all evidence supports it and there are no legitimate competing theories.

Pornography

Fundamentalists blame secular humanists for the wide availability of what they call "pornography and filth" in the United States. Although they never define pornography, it is clear that the content that they find disgusting and absent of any redeeming social value is sexually explicit displays, *i.e.*, one or more persons engaged in various sexual activities. It is obvious from the financial success of *Playboy*, *Penthouse*, *Hustler*, and a half dozen or so other "skin magazines," as well as the popularity of X-rated movies and home videos, that many adult Americans find enjoyment or satisfaction in this form of entertainment.

Secular humanists do *not* advocate or endorse the production and distribution of erotic magazines and films, but they do oppose any attempts to suppress such legitimate commerce. There are two important exceptions to this statement; sexually explicit materials that involve minor persons or depict any form of violence (called S&M formats) cannot be tolerated in a humane society and should be strenuously suppressed by mandated legal means. Because sexually explicit materials are suitable only for adult consumption (like tobacco products and alcoholic beverages), secular humanists believe that their sale and distribution should be appropriately restricted and regulated.

Two Views of Life

Abortion

Three propositions may be stated: (1) No organization or responsible individual advocates abortion as a routine means of birth control; (2) All reasonable people recognize that abortion must be an option available in certain cases, *e.g.*, rape, endangered maternal health, and when the fetus can be determined through diagnostic procedures to be incapable of human existence; (3) The primary causes of unplanned pregnancy are ignorance and carelessness, conditions that are remediable through comprehensive sex education programs in the schools and the availability of birth control techniques to sexually mature persons.

Secular humanists recognize that there is a world-wide population crisis, and a catastrophic problem in the U.S. with unplanned pregnancies among unmarried adolescents. Unwanted children constitute a human tragedy, as well as an enormous social and economic problem. Respect for life requires that society make provisions for the adequate care of all children, but humane concerns dictate implementation of educational programs designed to prevent unplanned conception. Sex education programs, preferably beginning in the elementary schools, must be supported by the local community before the last resort of abortion can be eliminated in all but medically determined cases.

Homosexuality

Fundamentalists argue that refusal by secular humanists to condemn homosexuality as a monstrous perversion and curse upon society is equivalent to approval of the practice and life style. They paraphrase Scripture to the effect that "if you are not against it, you are for it." Secular humanists do not advocate homosexuality or the gay life style as preferable alternatives, nor do they claim that homosexuality and heterosexuality are of "equal value," as Professor Webber suggests in one of his few intemperate remarks. Secular humanists recognize that, for whatever reasons, the gay life style is preferred by 5% to 10% of adult Americans.

It is wrong to deny the civil rights of a minority group just because their sexual preferences are difficult to understand. In fact, a recent survey found that 40% of Americans would vote for a homosexual candidate for President, assuming the person was otherwise qualified. Respect for individual differences is consistent with the best American tradition, and is virtually required by Christian ethics. It is worth noting that Jesus' personal orientation is by no means clear. He was never married, apparently fathered no children, and His close associates were all males.

Finally, returning to one of the questions initially posed, Who are the humanists? How widespread is the philosophy of humanism in the U.S.? By the most restrictive definition, *i.e.*, persons who are members of secular humanist organizations or subscribe to their periodicals, there are probably fewer than 100,000 secular humanists in the U.S. If, in addition, persons affiliated with Ethical Culture Societies, Humanistic Judaism, Unitarianism, and similar groups are included, hard-core humanists may only barely exceed one million. It is important to recognize that while fewer than 10% of American adults are atheists, another 25% or so could be classified as deists, because their theistic belief typically does not include a personal savior or any form of supernatural intervention in human affairs.

In addition, Christian humanists—who are certainly the vast majority of Christians in the U.S.—and most Jews and members of other non-Christian religious faiths subscribe to the central ethical principles of humanism. It can be concluded that while the majority of Americans do not accept the nontheistic elements of secular humanism, most American adults do hold secular views that are entirely consistent with humanistic philosophical principles.

Chapter 3

Tenets of Secular Humanism

It is apparent from letters to the editor and remarks by ultra-conservative politicians and fundamentalist preachers that there is much confusion about secular humanism. The basic tenets of secular humanism can be summarized in ten points.

Point 1

Secular humanists are committed to the ideal of individual freedom. This includes freedom from unnecessary governmental control as well as freedom of conscience and belief. At the cornerstone of human freedom are the inalienable rights of life, liberty, and the pursuit of happiness.

Point 2

Secular humanists endorse the full range of civil liberties for all people, including free speech, fair judicial process, religious liberty, freedom of association, and artistic, scientific, and cultural freedom. Also included is the individual's right to die with dignity.

Two Views of Life

Point 3

Secular humanists adhere to the principle of free inquiry. This means toleration of diverse opinions and respect for the right of individuals to express their beliefs, no matter how unpopular they may be. The principle of free inquiry applies to politics, morality, and religion, as well as to science and everyday life.

Point 4

Secular humanists endorse the philosophical tradition that maintains that ethics is an autonomous field of investigation. Human beings can cultivate and apply wisdom to achieve lives of virtue and excellence. Morality does not derive from divine authority.

Point 5

Secular humanists recognize the importance of religious experience in the lives of people, but deny that such experience has any supernatural basis. There is insufficient evidence for the claim that some divine purpose exists in the universe. The cosmos is best understood as the result of a natural process.

Point 6

Secular humanists are committed to the uses of rational methods of inquiry, logic, and evidence in developing knowledge and evaluating truth claims.

Secular Humanism

It is appropriate to look to the natural, biological, social, and behavioral sciences for knowledge about the origins of the universe and the evolution of the human species.

Point 7

Secular humanists regard the dignity and full development of the individual as a central value. All people should be encouraged to realize their creative talents and potentials. The individual right to universal education emanates from this value.

Point 8

Secular humanists endorse an educational process that is designed to develop an appreciation for moral virtues, critical intelligence, and the building of character. Moral education should foster the growth of ethical judgment and the capacity for responsible choice among alternative courses of action.

Point 9

Secular humanists believe that conservation of nature and respect for ecological relationships is a moral obligation. Destruction of the environment and exploitation of natural resources without careful consideration of the possible detrimental consequences for future generations is immoral.

Two Views of Life

Point 10

Secular humanists believe that nations of the world must renounce the resort to violence and force as a method of resolving disputes. Peaceful adjudication of differences by international courts and by the arts of negotiation and compromise is the only sane alternative.

In summary, secular humanists maintain that life is the preeminent human value, and reject all hypothesized supernatural causes and explanations. Secular humanism is a practical, everyday philosophy that has as its singular goal the enhancement of human earthly existence.

Readers interested in examining formal statements of secular humanist philosophy are referred to *A Secular Humanist Declaration* (1980) for a concise treatment and to Corliss Lamont's *The Philosophy of Humanism* (1982) for a detailed presentation. The primary journals of secular humanism are *The Humanist, Free Inquiry,* and *The American Rationalist.* These publications are available in most public libraries.

Chapter 4

Jesus' Ten Commandments

A prominent theme in U.S. Secretary of Education William Bennett's campaign to improve public education has been his advocacy of teaching values in America's schools. Key phrases in his rhetoric are "the achievement of moral literacy" and "the formation of character."

Virtually all Americans agree with Secretary Bennett on two points. First, as he claims. there is consensus on the traits that compose good character, *e.g.*, honesty, compassion, tolerance, and generosity. Second, Americans want these values expressed in school programs, both academic and extra-curricular.

The difficulty occurs when anyone attempts to organize desirable character traits into a systematic framework of ethical principles. Some people prefer the inculcation of absolute values, while others favor pedagogical approaches designed to develop moral reasoning capacity. Critics label the latter "situation ethics" or "moral relativism."

President Reagan proposed that the values that should be taught in schools are the "Judeo-Christian Ethic." Although he did not elaborate,

Two Views of Life

Mr. Reagan was probably referring to the well-known Ten Commandments found in Exodus and Deuteronomy. Despite widespread endorsement. these simple ordinances merely proscribe selected transgressions.

It is apparent to educators, theologians, and laypersons that the six "Thou shalt nots" do not make up an adequate basis for moral instruction. (The first four Commandments are theological directives.) What is required is not a series of specific dos and don'ts, but rather a set of ethical principles that constitute a foundation for proper living.

I suggest that Jesus' teachings as they are presented in the Gospel illustrate ten affirmative precepts that are unsurpassed as groundwork for moral education. Students of Scripture will be able to cite verses supportive of these principles, even though they are carefully stated in neutral language.

First, the universal human duty is to help other people. Everyone has a moral responsibility for the well-being and happiness of others.

Second, the obligation to assist others extends to persons who subscribe to different value systems. They deserve the same treatment as friends and family members.

Third, the only acceptable form of human interaction is peaceful in nature. There is never any justification for interpersonal aggression or violence.

Fourth, regardless of the misbehaviors other people may commit, no matter how serious the damage they may do, the only appropriate response is to forgive them.

Fifth, the goals in life that should be pursued are personal development and community service, rather than the acquisition of material possessions and wealth.

Sixth, criticism should be reserved for examination of one's own faults. No person is qualified to judge the motives of others.

Seventh, personal enjoyment is an important aspect of human existence. Ceremonies and celebrations that commemorate major events and milestone occasions give life meaning.

Eighth, spiritual and religious exercises, including prayer. are intensely personal activities that should be conducted in private to be truly meaningful.

Ninth, the compassionate society will be realized when self-interest becomes the standard by which concern for other people is measured.

Tenth, the infallible rule for monitoring individual behavior is the principle of anticipated reciprocity: we should behave toward others as we prefer to be treated.

Some readers will object that recommending Jesus' postulates as a basis for moral instruction is tantamount to teaching religion in the public schools, in violation of the First Amendment. Fortunately, Jesus' ethical truths can be separated completely from his theology. In other words, Jesus can be viewed as an insightful moral reformer and no more.

Furthermore, Jesus' precepts derive entirely from earlier teachers, including Confucius, Buddha, and Zoroaster, as well as several old Testament prophets, and are generally consistent with advice given by Augustine, Mohammed, and most secular philosophers beginning with Socrates. On specific issues of contemporary relevance, Jesus opposed materialism, militarism, capital punishment, and public prayer, while advocating pacifism, globalism, and moderate use of alcohol.

It is eminently reasonable to regard Jesus' ethical teachings as a convenient summary of society's accumulated moral wisdom. Jesus' ten commandments should be acceptable to persons of all religious faiths, and nonbelievers as well. I think that they provide an excellent foundation for moral instruction today.

Chapter 5

Jesus and Secular Humanism

Is there any common ground shared by fundamentalist Christians (FCs) and secular humanists (SHs)? Can persons affiliated with these two vastly different and competing systems of thought agree on anything? The extensive and often polemical writings generated by both groups would suggest that their views are at opposite poles on a philosophical continuum with absolutely no common points. FCs characterize SHs and their fellow travelers as immoral, un-American atheists who advocate socialism (or communism), while SHs generally regard FCs as irrational, ignorant political reactionaries who are racist, sexist, and anti-intellectual in their outlook.

FCs devoutly believe that the Bible is the inerrant word of God, both the Old and New Testaments, despite hundreds of contradictions, internal inconsistencies, and outright errors, and claim to base their lives on the absolute moral truths contained therein. In contrast, SHs (meaning roughly atheists, agnostics, rationalists, free-thinkers, and persons of similar persuasions) put their faith in the demonstrable strategies of modern scientific method. These individuals further subscribe to the proposition that rules of proper conduct or "moral truths" can be rationally derived and do not require divine inspiration for their validity.

Of course the basic difference between these two groups, which is the foundation for the emotional confrontations, lack of respect for each other, and even downright hatred of one another, is the disagreement about our ultimate fate. Does the human personality (called the soul by the FCs) transcend bodily death, or is physical death the end of existence for the individual? The underlying issue that separates FCs (and most other religious groups) from the SHs is belief in some form of everlasting "life" versus the conviction that this life is the only one. Hence, it follows that for SHs, life is the ultimate value, while for FCs eternity through salvation is the preoccupying concern and goal of life.

The mechanism that enables FCs and all persons of Christian faith to achieve everlasting life is postulated to be Jesus' death on the cross. Simply put, the basic axiom of Christianity is that if an individual accepts Jesus of Nazareth as personal Lord and Savior believing that He died for one's sins, then everlasting life with God, the Father in Heaven can be achieved. Needless to say, SHs reject this notion as silly and can't understand how anyone can possibly believe such an explanation. In fact, many SHs doubt that there was even an historical figure corresponding to the biblical Jesus, choosing to regard him as a mythical character like Socrates. In general, SHs and other skeptics deny the validity of Christian theology, including the miracles attributed to Jesus, and some or most biblical history. But Jesus' ethical teachings are an entirely different matter.

It is the thesis of this chapter that the major ethical teachings of Jesus that are presented in the Gospel are not inconsistent with the rationally-derived ethical principles of SH. If for the sake of argument we would define Christians as those persons who endorse and advocate adherence to Jesus' ethical teachings and no more, then most SHs could be called Christians! Or, we might suggest that if Jesus were to return tomorrow (a very reasonable possibility according to FCs) he would share numerous interests and concerns with SHs. Following this same line of argument it seems reasonable to suggest that SHs may share common ground and have points of agreement with their arch-enemies, the dogmatic, narrow-minded FCs.

Before accepting or rejecting this proposition suggesting a basis for rapprochement between FCs and SHs, we should first inspect Jesus' ethical teachings to assure ourselves that they are in the main acceptable to SHs. We assume that Jesus' teachings are acceptable to FCs, although as anyone who watches the Sunday morning evangelists sermonize knows, Jesus' ethical teachings receive scant attention. An excellent beginning point for this review is the Sermon on the Mount, which is regarded by most Christians, and many non-Christians as well, as the greatest ethical statement ever promulgated.

Before proceeding, two important qualifications should by emphasized. First, SH is not a unified doctrine and neither are SHs a homogeneous group. Each of the principles or viewpoints stated below is probably endorsed by the majority of SHs, but by no means all SHs. The philosophy of SH accommodates a wide diversity of opinions and positions. Second, as mentioned previously, many SHs deny that a man named Jesus lived. And even if he did there is no reliable evidence that he made the statements attributable to him in the Gospel. However, for the purpose of this chapter, it will be assumed that Jesus existed and that his views are accurately recorded in the Gospel.

Attitudes Towards One's Enemies

FCs and ultra-conservative politicians never tire of condemning the Soviet Union, characterizing it as an evil empire totally under Satanic influence. In contrast, the U.S. is described as a Christian nation richly blessed by Almighty God. Some reactionaries even advocate a first strike nuclear attack against the Soviet Union to end the imminent threat of atheistic communism and ultimate world domination. But Jesus was unequivocal about the proper attitude towards one's enemies. He said, "Some people say love your friends and hate your enemies, but I say love your enemies, help them, and pray for them." As staunch advocates of freedom, SHs emphasize their disagreements with Soviet Communism, condemning aggression in Afghanistan and numerous other Soviet misbehaviors, but realistically recognize the existing differences and recommend peaceful coexistence with the adversary. Jesus' ethical statement establishes a reasonable position that SHs can readily endorse.

On Capital Punishment

A basic tenet of FC social policy is embodied in one of Moses' rules for regulating interpersonal conduct, i.e., "an eye for an eye, a tooth for a tooth, and a life for a life." In fact, three-fourths of adult Americans endorse capital punishment as a suitable strategy for deterring serious crime and providing justice in the individual case. But, again, Jesus was perfectly clear about the issue. He contradicted Moses and other Old Testament prophets when he said, "Some people have said an eye for an eye, but I say when a person strikes you on the right cheek turn the left to him." Jesus taught that killing another person is wrong, even if it serves a societal sense of justice. SHs consider capital punishment to be legalized murder, the premeditated, intentional destruction of life. On the other hand, SHs strongly support appropriate punishment for crimes committed. But for SHs, life is the preeminent value and Jesus' ethical teaching cited above, as well as those principles discussed in the next two sections, are consistent with this position.

On Violence and Self-Defense

There is no recorded incident where Jesus actually engaged in violence or inflicted harm on any person. Nor did he ever advocate violence for any purpose, not even in defense of oneself. He can be legitimately regarded as a pacifist. (Some SHs may remember from early Sunday School indoctrination the story about Jesus chasing the money-changers out of the Temple with a whip, but there is no indication that he struck anyone.) When Pontius Pilate's soldiers came to arrest Jesus in the olive grove, Simon Peter cut off the ear of a slave boy who accompanied the group. Jesus admonished Peter to put away his sword and stated that "those persons who take up the sword shall perish by it." In other words, violence begets violence. Most SHs would entitle a person to use necessary force to defend self, family, and community, however. But the problem of violence in Christian America is endemic, permeating our printed material, television programming, movies, sports, and daily life. SHs can look to Jesus of Nazareth as an excellent role model for nonviolent behavior.

Concerning Forgiveness

Closely related to the problem of violence and self-defense is the doctrine of forgiveness. When the Pharisees brought an adulteress before Jesus and asked him if she was guilty of violating religious law, he declined to judge her saying, "let the person who is without sin cast the first stone." His general advice, found throughout the Gospel, is to forgive the transgressions of other people. To indicate the scope of a forgiving attitude, Jesus answered the question of how many times we should forgive someone with "not seven times, but 77 times seven." The ultimate example of forgiveness was provided by Jesus when he said of his executioners, "forgive them for they know not what they do." Although everyone knows how easy it is to diagnose the faults of other people and make harsh judgments about them, and conversely how difficult it can be to forgive the slightest insult or infraction, SHs can in principle certainly endorse Jesus' teachings in this matter.

On Acquisition and Possessions

The FCs would have us believe that free enterprise and capitalism are God's economic inventions. In fact, these forms of economic arrangements are utterly contradicted by Jesus' teachings. Conservative economists such as Milton Friedman state explicitly that self-interest, greed, or avarice drive the free enterprise system. Jesus recognized the corrupting effects of materialism and wealth when he advised the young man who sought salvation to "sell everything you have, give the proceeds to the poor, take up the cross and follow me." Jesus' logic is summarized as follows: "You cannot serve God and wealth—because a person cannot serve two masters, he or she will love one and hate the other." Of course, SHs do not advocate vows of poverty or exclusive, fanatic dedication to any single cause. Reasonable people desire enough to live happily and securely, but no more. For those who truly desire to follow Jesus' advice to the rich young man cited above, the Salvation Army provides a socially useful mechanism for serving the Lord.

Two Views of Life

Concerning Public Prayer

In comparison to truly important issues such as interpersonal violence and international relations, school prayer would seem to be of trivial significance in the overall scheme of things. But in the minds of the FCs, compulsory prayer in the public schools is of monumental concern. Silent prayer, which any child can engage in at any time, simply will not satisfy the FCs. Despite numerous rebuffs by various judicial bodies, including the U.S. Supreme Court, FCs will not yield in their insistence on required, audible prayer to begin the school day. For many reasons, all well known, SHs and the majority of religious people oppose legislated prayer in the public schools. But there would be no disagreement if we obeyed Jesus' teachings. He advised his followers not to make a public spectacle of prayer, but rather to make it a private, personally meaningful activity. Again, SHs find Jesus' advice eminently reasonable and a sound basis for public policy.

Concerning Good Works

An especially appealing aspect of FC doctrine is the axiom that salvation is by faith alone. FCs are adamant that no matter how meritorious, good deeds cannot justify the gift of eternal life. But FCs forget that salvation is contingent on *both* acceptance of Jesus as one's personal Savior *and* good works. Jesus expressed himself unequivocally on this issue: "Whenever you help people in need, you have helped me, and your reward shall be eternal life, but whenever you deny help to needy people, you have denied me, and your fate shall be everlasting punishment." Clearly, for Jesus both faith and humanitarian commitment are essential to achieving salvation. Of course, SHs recognize only the obligation to help their fellow humans, not because there is any ultimate reward for doing so, but because SHs respect the fundamental moral principle that teaches us to "love our neighbors as we love ourselves." So while their motives may be different, SHs and FCs would appear to be equally committed to the eradication of human suffering as the highest priority for a just society.

These seven issues certainly do not exhaust the possible areas of agreement between SHs and FCs. For example, moderate drinking of alcoholic beverages on festive occasions is supported by Jesus' first recorded miracle, in which he changed six pots of water to wine at a wedding feast in Cana. Also, Jesus vehemently opposed the practice of taking oaths on the Bible, stating that a person's word was sufficient for any purpose. It is important to emphasize that SHs do not agree with all of Jesus' teachings, and of course, SHs emphatically reject as barbaric most of the code of behavior presented in the Old Testament. But this qualification does not diminish the substantial areas of agreement that do exist for SHs and FCs. While it would be naive to expect the competing parties to entirely disregard their differences, it behooves SHs to emphasize the common ground whenever possible.

Chapter 6

Christian Humanism

This volume is appropriately dedicated to the memory of Rev. J. G. Bane, a person who exemplified the individual responsibility and social concern that characterizes Christian humanism. When he lived in Fayetteville, Arkansas, Rev. Bane devoted considerable time to writing letters on a variety of morally-relevant topics for publication in local newspapers. His carefully stated positions in the letters that compose this chapter constitute an excellent primer for Christian humanists.

Commitment Can End Abortion

I am glad that the Friday demonstrations in front of the Fayetteville Women's Clinic have stopped. While I agree with the protestors' goal of ending abortion in America, I do not think that the pro-life groups accomplish anything by harassing other people. In my opinion what is needed to address the abortion problem is constructive Christian action.

First, however, it is necessary for pro-life advocates to recognize that Dr. Harrison is not a "murderer of unborn children." They should realize that he is just as sincere in his beliefs as those who disagree with him. Jesus said repeatedly that we should not judge or condemn other people, lest we stand in judgment ourselves.

The vast majority of women who seek abortions do so because they don't think they have any acceptable alternatives. We must extend the Christian concept of homes for unwed mothers to all women with unwanted pregnancies if our goal is to stop abortion. But we must also be prepared to accept the financial burden for medical services and living arrangements for pregnant women and the babies that are born.

I don't think that financial limitations would be an obstacle to Christians in this matter. Congregations in Fayetteville and throughout Arkansas and the U.S. are spending huge amounts of money on themselves, building new churches, recreation facilities, family life centers, and even schools. If ending abortion in America is really the highest priority, then resources are available to implement the solution.

Who will assume responsibility for the infants? Mothers often decide to keep their previously unwanted babies. Tens of thousands of couples in U.S. cannot have children and badly want to adopt newborn infants. In the case of mixed race babies and those with physical and mental defects, however, there are seldom adoptive parents waiting. So Christians must be prepared to assume responsibility for this group of truly unwanted infants.

Marching, name-calling, and harassment will only serve to generate hostility and resentment, and may lead to violence. Neither will stronger laws or a constitutional amendment reduce the abortion rate. The problem of abortion in America can only be solved through Christian commitment to constructive action.

Commandments of the Christmas Spirit

As we prepare to celebrate the birth of Jesus of Nazareth, we should emphasize in our behavior the virtues that He taught us. Because Jesus' ethical teachings are similar to those of many other prophets, such as Buddha, Confucius, Zoroaster, Augustine, and Muhammed, as well as some latter day teachers, we should invite persons of all religious faiths to participate in the observance of Christmas.

We should also welcome Unitarians, agnostics, and humanists as well, because so many traditional aspects of our Christmas celebration have documented origins in the pagan religions of antiquity. December 25 was the major festival time for pagan religions that worshipped sun gods. The immediate precursor of the Christmas observance was the Roman Saturnalia, which antedated Jesus' birth by several hundred years.

In fact, early Christians observed Jesus' birthday on March 25, and it was not until the fourth century that Christmas was moved to December 25. Customs such as gift giving, family gatherings, decorating trees, and hanging holly and mistletoe all originated in pagan antiquity.

The true Christmas Spirit that derives from the ethical teachings of Jesus consists of three Commandments:

One, we should help people in need. Everybody should have adequate food, clothing, shelter, and medical attention. It is our Christian duty to eliminate all suffering. Salvation depends on our dedication to helping others.

Two, we should forgive other people for their transgressions against us, just as we hope to be forgiven ourselves. We should never harshly judge or condemn others. If we harbor any ill will toward our neighbors this is the season to resolve the differences.

Three, we should love our enemies. This means especially the leaders and people of the U.S.S.R. We must remember that they are sincere in their beliefs and proud of their nation. We should pray for their happiness and prosperity just as much as we pray for our own.

Put simply, the Christmas Spirit means behaving toward others exactly as Jesus taught us by His example some 2,000 years ago.

Two Views of Life

Evolution Does Not Contradict Christianity

The religious doctrine called creationism is apparently still alive and well in Arkansas, California, Louisiana, and several other states where legal challenges have been filed or are being planned. Some newspaper editorials and the recent flurry of letters to editors address the same old misconceptions, *i.e.*, evolution is only a theory, creationism should be given equal time, evolution is really a religious belief, and so on. I only wish that Christians would use a little common sense in these matters.

Darwinian evolution is the only scientific explanation of human origins. The vast majority of Christians accept this fact, of course. But a small, well-financed, vocal minority continues to embarrass the rest of us. John Anderson, the born-again presidential candidate in 1980, who had previously authored the infamous Jesus Amendment, provided a good example for all Christians. When asked during the election campaign if he thought the Genesis account of creation was literally true, he said, "Of course, not, it's just a religious story."

The Genesis account was concocted by Moses, who borrowed liberally from earlier creation myths, so that his people would have an answer to the ultimate question of how humans came into existence. It must also be recognized, of course, that the Old Testament accounts of Adam and Eve, the Fall, Cain and Abel, the Deluge, and Noah's Ark are also just religious stories. Christians should emphasize the *Who* and *Why* of creation and stop quibbling about topics that strike many Americans as just plain silly.

When Judge Overton, a Bible-believing, church-attending Christian himself, concluded that so-called "creation science" was not science at all, but rather religious dogma, that decision should have been sufficient for faithful Christians. Why not simply proclaim organic evolution to be God's divine mechanism of creation and recognize that Genesis presents only man's invented story? Surely, Almighty God can use random variation and genetic mutation to achieve his (or her) purposes!

Evolution does not contradict Christian faith. Science can only affirm true faith. It is time for responsible Christians to invest their resources and energies in projects that further the primary Christian goals of constructive action and social justice, as these are spelled out in the ethical teachings of Jesus.

Christians Are Obliged to Oppose Racism

Today is Martin Luther King Day, officially designated so by the Congress of the United States to honor one of our greatest Americans. He was a minister and social activist who exemplified in his life the teachings of our Lord and Savior, Jesus of Nazareth.

Christians should recognize Dr. King as possibly the greatest American in our nation's history, because he confronted the very worst evil in America, then and now, racism. (I fully realize that interpersonal violence and religious fanaticism are terrible problems, too.) Racism is the living legacy of slavery and segregation.

It is difficult to understand that slavery was officially abolished in America only 120 years ago and that segregation was ended just 30 years ago. But the virulent disease called racism continues undiminished. And this in a predominantly Christian nation that was founded on the central premise that *all people are created equal.*

Racism is a blot on the conscience of all Americans, but Christians have a special obligation and duty to carry on Dr. King's fight against bigotry and discrimination. Not surprisingly, the first official recognition of his birthday has been the occasion for an eruption of racist remarks and behavior. The worst by far was the statement attributed to a bank president in Eureka Springs, Arkansas, who said, "If we give the blacks a holiday, then the homosexuals will want one too." This man probably attends church services every Sunday.

Many Christians apparently don't know that Jesus was a Jew of Ethiopian heritage. Like most Semitic people of the time, He was dark-skinned with a protruding nose and oily black hair. If Jesus returned today He would look much more like Dr. Martin Luther King, Jr. than, say, Senator Jesse Helms or Rev. Jerry Falwell. And like Jesus, Dr.

King preached a consistent message of love and respect for all other human beings.

To commemorate his birthday, I call on all Americans to dedicate themselves to the ideals of human compassion, social justice, and common decency that motivated Dr. Martin Luther King, Jr.

Capital Punishment Violates Christianity

Like many Americans I am very disturbed by the increasing number of executions taking place in the United States. It is not just the government sponsored killings that are abhorrent, but even more distressing is the endorsement of capital punishment by some 80% of American adults. Taking human life under *any* conditions is completely contrary to the teachings of Jesus of Nazareth.

How can a nation that claims to be founded on a Christian moral tradition condone the barbaric practice of capital punishment? The answer can be located easily by turning to the Book of Deuteronomy in the Old Testament of the Judeo-Christian Bible. Here the main elements of Mosaic Law are given. It is well known, of course, that Moses borrowed extensively from earlier legal systems, especially the code of laws assembled by King Hammurabi of Babylon.

According to Mosaic Law the death penalty, usually carried out by stoning or crucifixion, is prescribed for the following crimes: advocating false religions, giving false testimony in capital cases, rebelliousness and drunkenness by youth, nonvirginity at marriage (for women only), adultery, and premeditated murder. The justification for the harsh penalty is two-fold: to eliminate evil by removing evil-doers and to deter others from committing evil acts.

The critical question for Christians is: What would Jesus say about this punitive, unforgiving legal tradition? We know that Jesus counseled forgiveness at all times. He said repeatedly that we should not judge or condemn other people, that we should not resist evil, and that we should not resort to violence, even in self-defense. And He gave us the ultimate example when He extended forgiveness to His executioners before He died. Should we stand up for Jesus or should we succumb to the primitive appeal of Hammurabi's Code?

I would also point out that all other Western democracies have outlawed capital punishment. This puts the United States in the company of the Soviet Union, South Africa, Iran, and Libya on this issue. How can we criticize these countries for human rights violations when we have institutionalized the most horrible violation of all, the intentional destruction of human life? Because America is a predominantly Christian nation, it is clear that we are killing in the name of Jesus.

I hope that Christians who advocate the death penalty will re-examine their thinking in this matter. A good place to start would be to study carefully the Gospel accounts of Jesus' life and teachings.

Secular Humanism

Principles of Christian Humanism

Congratulations to Fayetteville resident Rev. Thomas S. Vernon on publication of his book, *Unheavenly Discourses*. This well-written and interesting volume contains 12 chapters covering topics such as body and soul, sin, and the meaning of life. Because some Christian readers may find Rev. Vernon's conclusions confusing, I would like to summarize his main assertions and add my own brief clarifying comments.

1. Religious beliefs can imprison an unthinking person. How true. Faith requires the exercise of our critical intelligence.

2. The doctrine of biblical literalism is indefensible. True. Enlightened Christians have long ago rejected literalism.

3. Many people who believe the Bible to be infallible have not even read it. I am sorry to say this is true. What's more, a careful reading is a sure cure for biblical literalism.

4. Jesus' resurrection is not an established historical fact. Absolutely true; it is a matter of personal faith alone.

5. The concept of an eternal human soul is an implausible notion. Rev. Vernon is speaking as a philosopher rather than a theologian here.

6. The prospect of living forever in heaven is not particularly appealing. This is simply a personal view, but one that has merit.

7. The doctrine of original sin is a pernicious idea. There is much truth to this statement, because original sin is a negative assumption.

8. God is a figment of the human imagination. This could be true, because nobody has yet proved that God actually exists.

9. Proper human values do not depend on supernatural revelation. We must admit that this is true because many ethical and decent people are atheists.

10. Humanistic philosophy is not incompatible with belief in God. This is true, as evidenced by the many Christian humanists in our community.

11. The only really important sin is harming other people intentionally and unnecessarily. This is true because Jesus said so.

12. Religious faith entails a life-sustaining dependency on a supernatural being. This is a good definition of religious faith, one that deserves our careful examination.

13. Religion is necessary for some people, but not for other people. Absolutely true, a fine statement of the principle of Christian tolerance and respect for all people.

14. Humanism has become a catch-all label for sinfulness and evil in America. True, and abuse of people who subscribe to this philosophy is unchristian.

15. Meaning and purpose of life are human inventions. This is true, of course, and puts responsibility right where it belongs, directly on us.

I hope that this summary encourages everyone to read Rev. Vernon's fine book. It is thought-provoking and well worth the time invested. Rev. Vernon is trained in philosophy as well as in theology, so he really knows what he is talking about. He is also a humanist. Congratulations to him for an excellent book.

Part II

Radical

Fundamentalism

Introduction

The most salient feature of radical fundamentalism is its explicit religious bigotry. Fundamentalists are militantly intolerant of all other religious denominations, Christian and non-Christian alike. The basic axiom of radical fundamentalism is that there is only one true religion. All other belief systems represent false doctrine, and adherents of these heretical schemes will suffer eternal torment in hell.

Rev. Jimmy Swaggart is the unchallenged *Führer* of fundamentalist bigots. The following excerpts from his sermons convey the uncompromising, absolutist nature of fundamentalist malice toward other religions:

> Most religious people in the world are going to hell .... Religion is going to send more people to hell than anything else. . . Many churches preach poison ... Many of you will follow a preacher or priest to hell .... You've got to be born again ... You've got to come to Jesus ... Jesus is the only way.

Two central tenets of fundamentalism are inerrancy of Scripture and the innate human predilection for evil behavior. In defending the Genesis account of creation, Rev. Robert Dockery asked the rhetorical question, "Are Christianity and evolution compatible?" to which he answered, "Absolutely not! Belief in one precludes belief in the other! Either the Bible is true or evolution is! Both cannot be!" Illustrating the second tenet, Rev. H. D. McCarty wrote that ". . . ignorance of man's basic 'evil tendency' is the bedrock of all of our disappointments, delusions and unfulfilled expectations."

Fundamentalists call on their religious faith in practically any situation that arises. For example, Miss America of 1986, Kelleye Cash, revealed that members of her family held daily prayer sessions throughout the pageant. They believe that this gave Ms. Cash "an edge" over her competition. When Ms. Jerry Sherwood of St. Paul, Minnesota learned that a woman had been indicted for the beating death of Ms. Sherwood's 3-year-old boy more than 20 years earlier, she exclaimed, "I feel fantastic. I thank God. My son died wrongfully, and I hope the person responsible is going to pay. Maybe now he can rest in peace."

Part II contains six chapters. **Secular Humanism: America's Most Dangerous Religion** is an amusing illustration of fundamentalist hysteria about secular humanism. Next, a brief history of fundamentalism in the U.S. is presented in **Origins of Fundamentalism. Heresies of Fundamentalism** explains why radical fundamentalists are not Christians in any legitimate sense of the term. The fundamentalist prohibition against drinking is shown to be unbiblical in **Should Christians Drink Alco-**

holic **Beverages?** Surveys of religious people indicate that the question they would most like to ask God is, Why is there suffering? This conundrum is resolved biblically in **Why Do Innocent People Suffer?** Lastly, **Secular Humanism on Trial** summarizes two celebrated lawsuits brought by radical fundamentalists in conjunction with their ongoing campaign to christianize America.

Chapter 7

Secular Humanism: America's Most Dangerous Religion*

Today I am speaking on secular humanism, America's most dangerous religion. Most Americans today seem to be concerned and confused about what is happening in this good land. The conditions which led to the fall of the Roman Empire are being re-enacted before our very eyes. The goals which the communists have set for our destruction are taking place on schedule. What has produced the crisis of the hour? I am convinced, after much study and prayer, that one of the chief factors, and maybe *the* chief factor, contributing to the present darkness, crisis, and confusion in America is a new and sinister religion which has arisen on the scene. What is this religion? Secular humanism.

Why do I speak on this subject today? Because it is very evident that millions of Americans are either being taken captive or highly influenced by secular humanism. Our government is tremendously infiltrated with it. Our schools are being

---

* This Chapter consists of selected and edited segments from three sermons by Rev. Bill Bennett, former pastor of the First Baptist Church of Fort Smith, Arkansas.

56

dominated by it. It has creeped into the church. It is a major threat. One of our congressmen said that unless the American people arise by the millions that it will be the dominant religion in America very soon. And so God tells me to warn the people about this type thing; beware, be on your guard lest any man take you captive by philosophy and vain deceit, not after Jesus Christ. And that's the reason that I bring the message today, to inform and to warn and to point toward a solution.

What Is Secular Humanism?

For my information on secular humanism, I have drawn on their own manifesto: *Manifesto I*, published in 1933, and *Manifesto II*, published in 1973. I want to raise a few questions about secular humanism and seek to answer them. In the first place, what is secular humanism? In a word secular humanism is the belief that man is sufficient within himself and does not need God. Indeed man is God. Humanism is a man-made system that believes that man can help man without any help from God. Why is it called a religion? Because secular humanism directs itself to those beliefs and practices which are in living opposition to Judeo-Christian morality or our traditional values. Do you realize that the Supreme Court has defined secular humanism as a religion? It is a religion because it deals with those issues of life which religion addresses itself to. Why do we call it secular? Simply because of the meaning of the word secular—it's atheistic, it's anti-supernatural, it's anti-God.

Two Views of Life

The Philosophy of Secular Humanism

What are the chief beliefs of secular humanism? The first belief is that God is irrelevant. The second belief is that human reason is supreme. That man with his own mind can think out answers to the great problems which confront him in this day. Thirdly, that progress is inevitable, based on the evolutionary teaching that everything is progression—man and events are making progress all the time. The fourth general principle is that science is the guide to progress. They believe that progress comes only through science, nothing supernatural. No contribution from God whatsoever. In the next place they believe that man is completely autonomous. That is, that man is not under any restraint from any law or any ethic or anything except that which he thinks in his own heart. In their *Manifesto* they talk about maximum individual autonomy. Every man alone to himself. A sixth principle is that sin is not—it's just not a fact in human experience.

Now, based upon these principles, here are some specific things they believe. First, they do not believe in the existence of God. Secondly, they do not believe in the hereafter. Thirdly, they deny that the Bible is the word of God. In the fourth place they do believe in evolution, strongly. In the fifth place, they believe that every human being on the earth has complete sexual freedom. Maybe you are wondering where this came from to our society. That what a man prefers in the area of sex is his right and nobody's business, complete sexual freedom. All this I'm quoting from the *Manifesto*. In the next place, they believe that every individual regardless of age, has the right to determine his own goals and his own values and it's nobody's business but his. They also believe that every person in the world has a right to abortion.

Had you wondered how abortion has come into our society until within just 2 or 3 years we've murdered 6 million babies Secular humanism, that's exactly where it came from. That abortion is the right of anybody. Suicide is a right. You want to kill yourself? Kill yourself. And euthanasia? If they continue to make the inroads that they have been making in the last 10 years it may very well be that we won't have any old people around. They'll just eliminate them—euthanasia. And then they claim that there's no unchanging right or wrong in the Ten Commandments. Finally, they believe, not in national sovereignty, but in one-world government. These are some of their beliefs, the basic philosophy of secular humanism.

The Impact of Secular Humanism

How has secular humanism affected our lives, or how is it affecting our lives today? It has infiltrated every branch of the American government. For instance, the American Humanist Association was meeting in 1978 and the President of the United States sent them a telegram commending them "for greatly enhancing our way of life." Can you conceive of a person who claims to be a born again

Christian, reared in a Bible-believing denomination, who would commend an organization that is dedicated to destruction of the God he claims he knows? He may not have even known what he was doing, that's one of the sad things. Many people do not know about what's happened. The Vice-President of the United States is an avowed humanist, Walter Mondale. And his father signed *Humanist Manifesto I* in 1933. Secular humanism is reflected in law after law already on the books in America and there's quite a few laws pending in the Congress of the United States today which would embody secular humanism to the full.

Sometime ago the Swedish Parliament, and you would expect this to happen in Sweden, passed a law which virtually removed children from the control of their parents. Among other things it said no parent could spank a child. There is a law pending in the House of Representatives today that would accomplish the same thing in America. It would take your children from under your authority if it's passed. Senator Boren, who came over and spoke to us, said there was a school in the state of Washington getting money from the government through the HEW, and HEW informed them that they would have to cut off their funds unless they began to spank more girls. And so the school board was tied up on the question of whether to stop spanking boys that needed spanking and start spanking girls that didn't need any spanking.

Many of the strange things that have come into our ears today go right back to a secular humanistic philosophy. Alas, it has infiltrated our churches too much for me even to tell you today. Nelson Bell, the father-in-law of Billy Graham, before he died wrote an article that's been published far and wide, "The Great Counterfeit." What is "The Great Counterfeit"? He says the substitution of humanism for the Bible and for the Gospel in hundreds and thousands of churches in America. I was in a church just recently where the people told me that for 5 years their pastor (this was supposed to be an orthodox Southern Baptist Church) preached transactional analysis, whatever on earth that is. A very knowledgeable man at the National Affairs Seminar said that it is a rare thing indeed to find a preacher today who, Sunday after Sunday, preaches the Bible in his pulpit. Secular humanism has invaded the church greatly!

Secular Humanism and Public Education

But it seems that the chief inroad, indeed the chief inroad into our society, has been through public education. How has secular humanism invaded the domain of the public schools? Two ways chiefly. One, the secular humanists are educating our teachers today. Not all of them, but in the main they're educating our teachers. John Conlan told us that practically every teacher under the age of 35 had been given a heavy dose of secular humanism and, unless they were mighty informed and strong Christians, that many of them were teaching it in the public schools, week after week.

61

Some, he said, are teaching it who have no idea what it is and how destructive it is to Christianity and to our freedoms, to our families, to our churches, and to everything that we hold dear.

We have a crop of teachers now that have come up under the instruction of secular humanism. You say, well I wasn't taught that; well, if not, praise God, but I'm telling you what's a national trend today. But also, secular humanism has invaded our culture and society because they are writing the textbooks. The founder of a leading publishing house said, "Let me publish the textbooks and I care not who writes the music or makes the laws of a nation." And this is where secular humanism is coming in, through the textbooks.

The thrust of secular humanistic education is to train the child socially and psychologically—what is called behavioral modification—and not to stress equipment in skills and knowledge, reading, writing, arithmetic, the ability to think, but the emphasis is on behavioral modification and reorientation. This explains a lot of things that we are seeing in our culture today. Henry Morris says that evolution as a fact of science is being taught in practically all of our schools, even to the elementary children and he says the concept of the fall, of sin, of the curse, and of redemption are taboo. Through the teacher trained in secular humanism and through the textbooks being written by secular humanists, this philosophy has crept into America until it does or will soon dominate the entire public school system of America unless middle America wakes up to what is happening.

Secular Humanism and Communism

This country today stands in the most critical time of its entire history. Why is America in danger? America is in danger because her values are being eroded, denied and destroyed by godless secular humanism on the inside of this nation. But it's also in grave danger because it's being threatened by godless communism, both on the outside and the inside of the nation. It's amazing if you study the *Humanist Manifesto* and the *Communist Manifesto*, which I have been doing recently. I find that secular humanism and communism are very similar indeed; they are identical in their philosophy and their goals are basically the same.

Both deny the existence of God. The only difference is the communists are a little more honest, because they say they do not believe in God. The secular humanists say they are nontheist—a little more subtle. I find that communists are frugal and work and I discover that secular humanists often draw fat salaries from the establishment or the system they are trying to destroy. But we're talking about much of the same philosophy when we talk about communism. Dr. Schwartz said that secular humanism is the genus and that communism is the species. I want you to remember that. And communism is the major political expression of secular humanism.

Two Views of Life

When we talk about secular humanism and communism we are talking about the doctrines of demons and of hell. We're talking about that which challenges everything that's precious to you and your family. We're talking about a system that originated in hell and has been energized by the powers of darkness and there is no answer to it except the power of the Holy Ghost in the heart of the pastor and in the heart of deacons and in the heart of the Sunday school teacher and in the local church that can meet this tremendous darkening power that has descended upon the world. . . Oh I pray that you just won't receive this as information, but that you'll take it to an altar prayer, that you'll search out your soul because the lukewarm church is one of the greatest friends of communism and secular humanism.

Secular Humanism and Abortion

The support for abortion comes philosophically from the teaching of secular humanism. Secular humanism is the official religion of America today, not Christianity nor Judaism. If you want to know the fruit of secular humanism look at abortion and you'll see where secular humanism has led us. And what do they say about life? The secular humanists say there is no God or if there is a God He's irrelevant to life. They also say that man is no more than an animal and that his life is worth no more than a chimpanzee or a pig or a dog. They further say that man is responsible to no one but himself. It's no one's business what he does with his life. If he wants to take the life of an unborn child, that's his right. It's nobody's business. This is the philosophy that dominates the educational system of this land and dominates in the halls of Congress—this is the official religion of America.

What is abortion? Abortion is the taking of a life—killing, in most cases murder—to cover the sin of sexual immorality. I'm told by those who know that more than 90% of girls who ask for an abortion have been involved in fornication and sexual immorality. You see the Seventh Commandment says "Thou shalt not commit adultery." We have a generation today that has bought the humanistic philosophy and says we can commit adultery if we want to and we have many a teenage girl, unmarried, getting contraceptives and anything in the world so that she can be involved in immorality.

We're talking about one of the most serious problems in all the world. Where's the responsibility today? It's upon the pulpit, it's upon the church of Jesus Christ, to tell what the Bible says. It's to get the message to Congress and the Supreme Court to elect judges who don't believe in humanism. It's to get a president in the White House who doesn't believe in humanism. It's to tackle this thing and if the people of God don't do it, it's going to destroy us as a people. Something can be done and the only answer is the truth of the Lord.

Two Views of Life

Defeating Secular Humanism

What can you and I do? I just want to suggest several things as I close the message this morning. In the first place we desperately need to be grounded and rooted in the truth of the Bible. If you're a teacher you need to know what the Bible teaches or you could fall right into the trap and not even know it because it sounds like something great until you see it in the light of what the Bible really teaches. In the second place we desperately need to know the facts about secular humanism and that's the reason I'm preaching today on it. I want to encourage every teacher and every school administrator to get a copy of the *Humanist Manifesto I* and *II*. Please get a copy and read it for yourself. In the third place we need to understand the nature of the battle. Now we have a lot of conservative groups in America that recognize the problem, but they don't understand the nature of the battle. The battle is spiritual and that's the reason I'm preaching on it this morning. The battle is the battle of the church and of the people of God. It's a battle against Satan and darkness.

As Paul says in Ephesians, our fight is not against a physical enemy, but we are up against the unseen powers of darkness which control this world and spiritual agents from the very headquarters of hell. We're up against Satan and the powers of the devil and we have got to recognize it for the problem that it is. And then finally, we've got to get right with God and stay right with Him. Listen, we cannot fight the battle that is before us unless we are concerned and unless we absolutely are willing to stand up in the power of God and fight the enemy. Our nation today needs healing all over. It needs healing spiritually, it needs healing psychologically, it needs healing physically, economically, educationally, and politically. God tells us how healing can come to a nation. It can come only through God's people getting right with God and staying right with God. The church has got to repent. The church has got to get right with God if we are going to stem the tide of secular humanism.

We have to stand up or secular humanism will destroy us. It is destroying us at this hour. Will you be a part of the problem or a part of the solution? Beware, see to it that you're not taken captive by secular humanism and taken as a spoil of war. Many of our students today have been taken captive. I've seen them come back from college since I've been here in this church and they were not just influenced. I've seen students who've been taken captive. They've been claimed as booty by the devil. Their minds have been captured by an alien, godless philosophy, secular humanism. It's high time that we rose up. Middle America can absolutely call a halt to it, but it's going to take millions of us, millions of us. What are you going to do about this problem?

Chapter 8

Origins of Fundamentalism

At the beginning of the twentieth century America was for all practical purposes a Christian nation. The vast majority of citizens were professing Christians. Prayer and Bible-reading were accepted activities in public as well as in private life. Most Americans believed that God's will was expressed in democracy, capitalism, and individual achievement.

But the seeds of dissension in this nominally Christian nation had already been planted by 1900. The ultra-conservative religious movement subsequently named fundamentalism was separating from mainline evangelical Protestantism. Fundamentalism emerged in reaction to liberal theology, which was attempting to accommodate Christianity to scientific, intellectual, and theological developments occurring at the time. By far the most disturbing ideas were those of scholarly biblical criticism and Darwinian evolution.

The doctrinal foundation of fundamentalism was expounded in a series of 12 paperback volumes published between 1910 and 1915. Titled *The Fundamentals*, the booklets covered a range of topics including the defense of inerrancy, an attack on biblical scholarship, and polemics against Mormonism, Catholicism, and Christian Science, as well as discussions of traditional theological issues such as the nature of the Trinity. The term "fundamentalist" was coined in 1920 to refer to people who identified themselves with theological positions detailed in *The Fundamentals*.

The central dogma of fundamentalist theology is the absolute accuracy or "inerrancy" of Scripture. Fundamentalists regard the Bible as an infallible source of religious and moral authority. Subsidiary postulates include the deity of Jesus, His virgin birth, His substitutional atonement for the sins of humankind, the authenticity of His miracles, His bodily resurrection, and His visible return or Second Coming. For fundamentalists, the Second Coming is formalized in the doctrine of premillennialism, the belief that Jesus will return to earth (soon) to institute a reign of 1,000 years of peace before the final cataclysmic end of the world.

The fundamentalist movement was basically an emotional response to the accelerating scientific and industrial progress that occurred after the Civil War. Fundamentalism developed into an all encompassing world-view, extending from religious dogma to morality and society. Fundamentalists were opposed to drinking, dancing, gambling, card playing, attending movies, and various other "sinful" activities. Charismatic preachers like Dwight Moody, William Jennings Bryan, and Billy Sunday spread the extremist gospel of fundamentalism.

Two Views of Life

Fundamentalists fought and ultimately lost two major battles early in the twentieth century that permanently shaped the public image of fundamentalism. The first was their long-cherished goal of making the manufacture or sale of liquor illegal in the U.S. Ratification of the Eighteenth Amendment to the Constitution in 1919 imposed Prohibition on all Americans and gave fundamentalists their greatest victory. (Prohibition was repealed in 1933 with passage of the Twenty-first Amendment.) Despite the failure of the "great experiment," fundamentalists still regularly oppose liquor-by-the-drink proposals in several midwestern states.

The second battle that fundamentalists fought was against the teaching of Darwinian evolution in the public schools. Evolution was considered to be a heretical formulation because it directly contradicted the most basic dogma of fundamentalism, inerrancy of the Bible. If evolution was right, the biblical account of creation was clearly erroneous. Hence, the monumental importance to fundamentalists of the "monkey trial" in Dayton, Tennessee in the summer of 1925.

During the preceding decade, fundamentalists had successfully enacted anti-evolution laws in several Southern states. John Scopes, a high school biology teacher, was indicted for violating Tennessee's law against teaching Darwinian theory. In one of the most celebrated and publicized judicial proceedings of the time, Clarence Darrow made a fool of William Jennings Bryan and his fundamentalist supporters. Darrow's performance was instrumental in permanently shaping the popular view of fundamentalists as reactionaries and buffoons. Fundamentalism has never recovered from the fiasco of the Scopes trial.

In addition to their battles against liquor and evolution, fundamentalists were involved in three other damaging struggles. They opposed the social gospel movement, which advocated socialism as the Christian alternative to capitalism, because they equated socialism with "Godless atheistic communism." Because fundamentalists were allied with the Ku Klux Klan in the South, they opposed a plank condemning the Klan at the Democratic national convention in 1924. Finally, they opposed the nomination of Alfred E. Smith for the 1924 presidential nomination because he was a Catholic.

During the 50-year period beginning in 1875 fundamentalism emerged from respectable traditions of revivalism and evangelicalism and acquired a thoroughly independent identity. By 1925 fundamentalists had become completely alienated from mainline Protestantism and isolated from mainstream American culture. There is consensus among religious historians that fundamentalism was a national laughingstock by 1925. Fundamentalism appealed primarily to uneducated people with racist attitudes, lack of self-respect, personal fear of damnation, and hatred for other religious belief systems.

Two Views of Life

Apart from the Christian anti-communist crusades conducted by Carl McIntire, Billy James Hargis, and Gerald L. K. Smith (constructor of the Christ of the Ozarks statue), fundamentalism was essentially dormant for a half century. In the 1970s "born again" Christians became active in politics, supporting Jimmy Carter's campaign for president. Encouraged by his surprising success, a coalition of Protestants from Baptist and Pentecostal denominations aligned with conservative Catholics and organized to elect Ronald Reagan.

The highly visible leaders of the neo-fundamentalist political strike force included Jerry Falwell, Tim LaHaye, Jimmy Swaggart, James Robison, Pat Robertson, Jim and Tammy Bakker, Richard Viguerie, Phyllis Schlaffly, William F. Buckley, Patrick Buchanan, and Robert Bauman. Almost every "moral issue" that the resurgent fundamentalists raised in the 1980s had been raised by their predecessors almost a century earlier. Abortion is the one notable exception to this historical continuity.

Some examples of political themes of contemporary fundamentalism that can be directly traced to the earlier period are: the claim that America is a Christian nation, militant nationalism and patriotic extremism (exemplified by Gerald L. K. Smith's newspaper called *The Cross and the Flag*), opposition to social programs to help poor people, the goal of Christianizing America through mandatory Bible teaching and prayer in the public schools, vicious attacks on all nonfundamentalist religions

72

(especially Catholicism, Judaism, and Mormonism), and paranoia concerning they bogeyman of one-world government (in 1919 fundamentalists opposed the U.S. joining the League of Nations).

One of the three central issues in neo-fundamentalist social theology, rivalled only by the misnamed pro-life movement and compulsory school prayer, is anti-evolution. Fundamentalist strategy now is not to eliminate teaching of evolution from the schools, however, but rather to balance the presentation by giving equal time to creationism. Lower courts have ruled that "creation science" laws in Arkansas and Louisiana violated the U.S. Constitution by requiring the inculcation of religious creationist dogma in the public schools. In June, 1987, the U.S. Supreme Court ruled the Louisiana law unconstitutional.

Demonstrating the scientific consensus about evolution, which is *the* unifying principle of the life sciences, 72 Nobel Prize recipients in science and 24 scientific organizations filed a brief with the Supreme Court urging rejection of the Louisiana appeal for the simple reason that creationism is not legitimate science. Yet, opinion polls continue to show that the majority of adult Americans think that both explanations of origins should be taught in biology classes. Politicians fully appreciate and readily exploit public misunderstanding of this subject. Governor Bill Clinton and U.S. Secretary of Education William Bennett, both lawyers, have expressed the opinion that local school boards should decide whether "creation science" is included in the curriculum.

Psychiatrists, psychologists, sociologists, historians, and political scientists have studied fundamentalism and reached essentially the same conclusions. Their findings can by summarized in four interrelated points.

First, fundamentalists are distrustful of intellectual approaches to knowledge and life. They manifest a superstitious resistance to science, preferring absolute answers to life's questions, rather than tentative scientific formulations. Psychologists refer to this syndrome as intolerance for ambiguity, which derives from fear of uncertainty.

Second, fundamentalists adhere rigidly to traditional values and standards, which are viewed as sacred and immutable. They insist on strict enforcement of rules and severe punishment for violators. Their cynical view of human nature is expressed in a suspicious and distrustful attitude toward other people. Fundamentalists' moralistic sexual perspective betrays feelings of insecurity and inferiority.

Third, fundamentalists identify with powerful authority figures to whom they are unquestionably obedient. This uncritical acceptance of their moral leaders' directives and judgments produces a narrow identification with their leaders' views and results in stereotypic portrayals of competing belief systems. The need to submit oneself totally to authority is a reflection of personal weakness and low self-esteem.

Fourth, fundamentalists are aggressively intolerant of religious and political perspectives that conflict with their beliefs. Anyone who disagrees with fundamentalist dogma is immediately labelled un-American, unchristian, satanic, a communist, or worst of all, a secular humanist. Fundamentalists are cognitively inflexible and egocentric, lacking personal autonomy or independent judgment capacity, and they are fearful of societal change.

Chapter 9

Heresies of Fundamentalism

The most serious allegation that can be brought against fundamentalists is that they are not Christians. To evaluate the validity of this charge it is necessary to define exactly what it means to be a Christian. Most Christian theologians would accept the following as essential doctrine: Christians accept Jesus Christ as their Lord and Saviour, believing He died for their sins so that they can attain everlasting life.

Can Christians achieve salvation through personal faith alone? Acceptance of Jesus as one's personal Saviour is certainly *necessary* to be saved, but is it *sufficient*? The answer to this question is clearly no. Jesus stated repeatedly that His followers were obligated to obey His teachings (*e.g.*, see Matthew 28:20 and John 14:21). But even if Jesus had not said so, common sense dictates that "accepting Jesus as Lord and Saviour" implies obedience to His ethical precepts.

Because salvation by faith alone is axiomatic among fundamentalists, a brief digression is necessary to document scripturally the insufficiency of this erroneous premise. We can turn to Jesus Himself for the clearest statement of the relation-

76

ship between good works and salvation. Jesus said that when the Messiah returns to make the Final Judgment, righteous people will be separated from the cursed on the basis of their conduct toward their neighbors, with the former achieving everlasting life and the latter eternal punishment (see Matthew 25:31-46). Additional supporting verses are Matthew 5:16, Matthew 16:27, John 14:12, John 15:16-17, and Romans 2:5-8.

Jesus' most basic ethical teaching is that we should love other people just as much as we love ourselves. Surely, for fundamentalists this injunction would extend to Christians, as well as to all other people. Yet, it is obvious from their public statements and behavior that fundamentalists only love other fundamentalists. For example, Rev. Jimmy Swaggart stated a generally accepted fundamentalist view: "There aren't many good churches in this land. . . You better find yourself a tongue-speaking, Holy Ghost inspired church if you want to be saved. . . There is only one way to worship the Lord. . . It's Jesus Christ or it's Hell."

Needless to say, Rev. Swaggart and other fundamentalist evangelists do not restrict their animosity and condemnation to religions outside the Judeo-Christian tradition, such as Buddhism, which they regard as equivalent to atheism. And it should also be apparent that Jews cannot be saved, because they don't accept Jesus as Lord and Saviour or believe that He was God. Rev. Swaggart, Rev. Tim LaHaye, and the infamous Tony Alamo of

Alma, Arkansas have declared Catholicism to be a false religion (and much worse).

Fundamentalists have long characterized Mormonism, Christian Science, Seventh Day Adventism, and Jehovah's Witnesses as "cults," along with newer Christian sects such as the Unification Church and the Worldwide Church of God. Fundamentalist preacher Rev. H. D. McCarty suggested that the "liberal" Protestant churches were responsible for divorce, adultery, drug abuse, and homosexuality. Suffice it to say that fundamentalist leaders do not express much love for their nonfundamentalist Christian neighbors.

Nor should it be too surprising that fundamentalist televangelists occasionally attack each other. For example, Rev. Garner Ted Armstrong has accused "rival religious organizations" that are aligned with "satanic forces" of trying to squeeze his program off the air be offering TV stations more money for the most desirable times. Rev. Swaggart has often ridiculed a positive coping strategy called "possibility thinking" promoted by Rev. Robert Schuller, an upbeat, optimistic TV preacher who disdains the hellfire and damnation approach that Swaggart favors.

If fundamentalists find it impossible to obey Jesus' commandment to love our neighbors, how might they behave toward their enemies? In the Sermon on the Mount, Jesus instructed us to love our enemies, help them, and pray for them. Yet, unbelievably, an increasingly popular practice among fundamentalists is to pray for the deaths of their enemies! This terrible tradition began a few years ago when Rev. Bob Jones, Sr. led the Bob Jones University student body in praying for the death of Alexander Haig, who was then U.S. Secretary of State and is a Catholic. To earn the wrath of God, Secretary Haig had refused to allow Irish Protestant hatemonger Rev. Ian Paisely to enter the U.S. to attend a Board of Trustees meeting at BJU.

Rev. Greg Dixon, who heads the Indianapolis Baptist Temple, has institutionalized the practice of praying for the deaths of enemies. His Courts of Divine Justice are being set up around the U.S. for the purpose of "convicting" opponents and praying that they die and be "delivered into God's hands." When Supreme Court Justice William Brennan delivered a commencement address in Los Angeles, Rev. L. L. Hymers exhorted his congregation at the Fundamentalist Baptist Tabernacle to pray for Justice Brennan's death (because Brennan supported the 1973 decision legalizing abortion).

Apparently fundamentalists don't have much confidence in the efficacy of prayers directed against the satanically-inspired Soviet menace. Just in case their prayers fail, fundamentalists are uncompromising advocates of militarism, a position diametrically opposed to Jesus' teachings. Jesus was the ultimate pacifist, condemning violence in all circumstances, including self-defense. He counseled us to love our enemies and to forgive those who harm us. This is presumably why we call Jesus the "Prince of Peace" every Christmas.

Two Views of Life

The fundamentalist political organization now called the Liberty Federation (previously the Moral Majority) selected the 10 best members of the U.S. House of Representatives in 1986. The choice was based on representatives' votes on six key "moral issues," including aid to the Nicaraguan contras and support for the MX missile. The Christian Voice, another right-wing lobbying outfit, issued its annual Biblical Scorecard, giving ultra-conservative Senatorial candidate Asa Hutchinson a rating of 92 for opposing nuclear reduction and favoring increased military spending, with special emphasis on the far-fetched "Star Wars" scheme. (Hutchinson is an alumnus of Bob Jones University.)

Fundamentalist military advocacy was symbolized in the annual God and Country Service at the First Baptist Church in Little Rock where presidential aspirant Rev. Pat Robertson sermonized the patriotic congregation. The celebration was highlighted by a color guard of four Junior Reserve Offices Training Corps cadets marching down the aisle of the sanctuary carrying flags and bearing rifles. Rev. Robertson has stated many times that fundamentalists are more patriotic than other citizens. He apparently equates patriotism with militarism.

Following the murderous U.S. bombing raid on Libya, in which scores of civilians were killed or injured, fundamentalist preachers across the nation applauded the action as an appropriate strategy to combat terrorism. In the Fayetteville area, Rev. H. D. McCarty assumed responsibility for outlining the fundamentalist moral position on war. He concluded that until Jesus triumphs we will have to continue to use lethal force against our enemies. It is patently clear to students of the Gospel that Jesus cannot triumph until Christians obey His commandments.

Fundamentalist positions on many other so-called moral issues flatly contradict Jesus' teachings. A long-standing goal of fundamentalists is to implement compulsory prayer and religious invocations in public schools and governmental assemblies. Yet, Jesus was unequivocal in instructing us not to make a public spectacle of prayer as the hypocrites do, but rather to make prayer a personally meaningful and private activity.

A unifying catch-phrase in much fundamentalist rhetoric is "pro-family." Yet, Jesus exemplified what are now called Christian values in His perfect life, which did not include marriage or children. An in one truly memorable statement, which must trouble biblical literalists, Jesus said that His objective was to cause disharmony between children and parents and ultimately, to disrupt and destroy the nuclear family. (Of course, we know that Jesus was simply indicating that His followers must renounce earthly attachments and commit their lives to Him.)

Briefly, a few other examples of fundamentalist heresies are: condemnation of consumption of alcoholic beverages (Jesus was by His own admission a moderate drinker and clearly approved of the practice), advocacy of capitalism as God's choice among economic systems (Jesus advocated a communal lifestyle that emphasized rejection of materialism and stressed the importance of helping others), and endorsement of the death penalty for murder, adultery, and homosexuality (Jesus commanded us to forgive other people without exception).

It is obvious to even the casual observer that major fundamentalist positions on social and political issues contradict Jesus' commandments. This is the basis for the conclusion by numerous Protestant theologians and clergy that fundamentalism and Christianity are antithetical belief systems. It is ironic that the fundamentalists' most hated enemy, the secular humanists, endorse Jesus' prescriptions for civilized living.

A theologically meaningful definition of Christian faith must incorporate the ethical teachings of the The Saviour. Followers of Jesus should obey His commandments and strive to implement His teachings in domestic social programs and in U.S. foreign policy. In other words, true Christians model their lives after Jesus' perfect example. The cure for heretical fundamentalism is simply to study the Gospel account of Jesus' life and teachings, rather than listening to blasphemous fundamentalist preachers.

Chapter 10

Should Christians Drink Alcoholic Beverages?

Anybody who lives in the American Bible Belt knows very well the fundamentalist Christian position on alcoholic beverages. Whether beer, wine, or liquor, any person who touches a drop of the Devil's elixir is committing a terrible sin and risks eternal Hellfire. Many communities in the Bible Belt are bone "dry" as the result of voter preference—there are no liquor stores, no taverns, and no night clubs. Nor do grocery stores or restaurants sell alcoholic beverages.

According to fundamentalist preachers, ranging from the big name TV evangelists like Rev. Jerry Falwell and Rev. Jimmy Swaggart down to local backwoods ministers of the Gospel, the Bible absolutely prohibits the consumption of alcoholic beverages. But when the curious person searches Scripture for the relevant verses, all that can be found is some two dozen proscriptions against drunkenness. Concerning the seriousness of this social problem, humanists, rationalists, and atheists agree wholeheartedly with fundamentalists. But what about moderate drinking?

Two Views of Life

John (2:1-10) recorded the first miracle that Jesus performed, which took place at a wedding feast in Cana of Galilee in the presence of Jesus' mother and His disciples. After the supply of wine was exhausted by the revelers, at the request of His mother, Jesus transformed six pots of water into wine. Obviously, Jesus did not consider the appropriate use of alcoholic beverages to be sinful. Although John did not say so, it would be unreasonable to think that Jesus did not participate in toasts to the bride and bridegroom and otherwise imbibe some of the product of His miracle.

Fortunately, fundamentalists and other Christians do not have to rely on the reasonable judgment of secular humanists in this matter. No less an authority than Rev. Garner Ted Armstrong, in his monumental study, *The Real Jesus*, states that there is no doubt whatever that Jesus drank wine at the celebration in Cana. Furthermore, Rev. Armstrong concluded that Jesus enjoyed a glass of wine on regular occasions.

Clearly, then, there is no biblical basis for the fundamentalist prohibition against any and all use of alcohol. But what about the modern medical position? Popular medical advisors like Dr. Timothy Johnson and the Mayo Clinic Health Letter are reluctant to prescribe moderate consumption of alcoholic drinks as a general health practice, even though epidemiological evidence supports such a recommendation. Regardless, common sense and Jesus' personal behavior suggest that a sensible Christian stance recognizes the benefits of appropriate and moderate use of alcoholic beverages.

Chapter 11

Why Do Innocent People Suffer?

Because it is confined mainly to an intensely disliked segment of the U.S. population, AIDS has provoked considerable discussion and speculation among religiously motivated writers.

Fundamentalist ministers such as Rev. Charles Stanley of Atlanta and Rev. David Baxter of Morrilton, Arkansas, and ultra-conservative columnists like Patrick Buchanan and William F. Buckley, have declared that AIDS is God's punishment for homosexuality.

And while about three-quarters of AIDS victims are gay males, with most of the remainder being intravenous drug users, a small fraction of AIDS patients are adults and children who contracted the disease through contaminated blood transfusions.

A well-known example of a person in the latter category is 12-year old hemophiliac Ryan White of Kokomo, Indiana, whose parents have been fighting a lengthy battle just to enable him to attend public school.

Many religious people wonder why an all-powerful God would allow Ryan White and a few hundred other entirely innocent individuals to become infected with AIDS. More generally, why doesn't God restrict punishment to sinners and evil-doers?

Examples of apparent injustice go beyond AIDS to infants born with monstrous defects and malformations, decent people who are severely disabled in terrible accidents, and God-fearing individuals who are afflicted with cancer, stroke, multiple sclerosis, and other devastating diseases. Why?

Eminent theologians such as Augustine, Luther, Calvin, Kierkegaard, and Schweitzer, as well as popular authors like C. S. Lewis and Rabbi Harold Kushner have all addressed this seemingly unfathomable subject. Despite praiseworthy efforts nobody has given a truly satisfactory answer.

For fundamentalists the resolution to this moral conundrum is found in Exodus 20:5, where God explains that punishment for disobeying His commandments may extend to the children, grandchildren, and great grandchildren of the sinner.

In other words, when innocent persons suffer from incurable diseases or traumatic accidents, we can reasonably and properly conclude that they are justly paying for the sins of their parents, grandparents, or great grandparents. This may seem unfair, but it is God's law.

Two Views of Life

The clear implication is that our misbehavior and sinfulness can have horrible consequences for future generations. For readers who require gruesome details, God's punishments, which include parents cannibalizing their children, are spelled out in Leviticus 26:14-39.

Chapter 12

Secular Humanism on Trial

Two widely reported courtroom dramas that took place in 1986 resulted in two commendable accomplishments. A virtually unknown philosophy called secular humanism received national media attention far beyond its adherents' greatest hopes. At the same time, radical fundamentalism was exposed as a malignant form of antediluvianism and a prime source of religious bigotry in the U.S. In federal court trials in Greenville, Tennessee and Mobile, Alabama fundamentalist fanatics attacked and condemned every idea that is inconsistent with their eccentric interpretation of the Word of God.

Roots of Intolerance

In the Tennessee case, seven fundamentalist families sued the Hawkins County School Board, claiming that a series of reading texts published by Holt, Rinehart, and Winston violated their First Amendment rights to free exercise of religion. Among the more than 400 specific objections to the Holt books that the parents cited were many that revealed clearly the disturbed nature of the fundamentalist mentality.

8

Two Views of Life

The parents' complaints about "Cinderella," "The Wizard of Oz," and "Macbeth" were merely laughable. But objections to "The Diary of Anne Frank," because it contains the suggestion that all religions are equally valid, and to reading about Catholicism, Islam, and American Indian religions, because this could confuse their children's thinking, are testimony to the absolute intolerance for other belief systems that is inherent in fundamentalism.

Not surprisingly, the plaintiffs objected to stories about dinosaurs, if the creatures were said to be older than the Genesis account of creation would allow. Any criticism of the free enterprise system was unacceptable because "capitalism is ordained by God." An, of course, any depiction of girls engaging in traditionally boys' activities such as carpentry was deemed inappropriate, because "God meant for women to be subservient to men."

In general, the parents argued that the "heathen" Holt series was "polluted" with stories advocating magic, feminism, pacifism, gun control, evolution, situation ethics, and one-world government, all of which are alleged by fundamentalists to be manifestations of the Satanic doctrine of secular humanism.

Unbelievably, U.S. District Judge Thomas G. Hull ruled that because the plaintiffs' "sincerely held religious beliefs" were entitled to constitutional protection, the school board had the obligation to provide an alternative educational experience that was not offensive to the parents. However, Judge Hull did not grant the parents' request that they be allowed to select different textbooks; rather he suggested that the parents could teach reading to their children at home.

It might just be that the proffered remedy could have been the ultimate cure for the parents' meddling interference with the instructional program! Unfortunately, Judge Hull later reinforced the plaintiffs' religious prejudice by awarding them $50,000 as reimbursement for the cost of sending their children to private schools during the dispute.

It is ironic that some of the Holt Basic Readers that the families found so objectionable were being used at Jerry Falwell's Lynchburg Christian Academy. Another interesting item of information was the revelation that the lawyer for the parents had asked the Ku Klux Klan to postpone plans to march during the trial in support of the parents, because he was worried about the unfavorable impression that would be created.

Significantly, the strongest condemnations of Judge Hull's decision were published by ultra-conservative columnists and politicians. Secretary of Education William Bennett said that the ruling was "a mistake"—that just because parents don't agree with everything in the curriculum does not give them the right to remove their children from class. George Will characterized the decision as judicially mandated censorship of offensive ideas and a wholly unwarranted extension of First Amendment protection to the domain of sectarian beliefs. William Buckley, Jr. was similarly unenthusiastic about the Tennessee ruling.

The central issue for public education raised in the parents' complaints is that of the fundamentalists' militant intolerance and total lack of respect for the religious beliefs of other Americans. The parents objected to all ideas and concepts that they considered to be inconsistent with their highly selective, idiosyncratic reading of Scripture. Their basic premise is that there is only one true religion, and all others are heretical and therefore should be suppressed.

Fortunately, fundamentalist bigots constitute only a small minority of the U.S. adult population. A survey conducted shortly after Judge Hull's decision was announced found that 80% of American adults approve of courses or units of instruction in the public schools that teach about the major religions of the world, while only 16% object. Even George Bush, who is well known for kowtowing to fundamentalists, bravely told a convention of religious broadcasters that there is no reason that children shouldn't read "The Diary of Anne Frank."

A happy ending to the Hawkins County school saga came about in August, 1987, when the United States Court of Appeals reversed Judge Hull on all counts, including the award of damages, and remanded the case with directions to dismiss the complaint. On February 22, 1988, the United States

Supreme Court declined to review the ruling of the court of appeals.

Inhibition of Christianity

In 1983, federal district Judge W. Brevard Hand upheld the constitutionality of an Alabama law that authorized daily moments of silence for prayer or meditation in the public schools. In early 1986 the U.S. Supreme Court overturned the law, ruling that it was a violation of the First Amendment.

However, in a footnote to his original decision (suggesting that he anticipated reversal on appeal), Judge Hand indicated that if he was overruled he would then consider whether various doctrines such as evolution, socialism, and secular humanism were being taught in the public schools in violation of the U.S. Constitution.

True to his word, Judge Hand set up a case in the summer of 1986 to continue his judicial battle against Godless humanism. The plaintiffs, 624 fundamentalist parents and teachers, claimed that secular humanism is equivalent to a religion and, therefore, cannot be taught in the public schools. They charged further that the curriculum used by the Mobile County school system caused the "unconstitutional inhibition of Christianity."

At the trial testimony was given on behalf of the plaintiffs to document that secular humanism is a religion, that it pervades the textbooks adopted in

Two Views of Life

Mobile County, and that the Christian religion is excluded from the curriculum. It was noted by the defendants, the Alabama State Board of Education and 12 parents, that fewer than 50 of the 4,000 textbooks approved by the state textbook selection committee were actually challenged by the plaintiffs.

Most of the testimony in the Alabama case addressed two major questions. Is secular humanism a religion that is being taught in the schools? Is the role of religion in history systematically censored from public school textbooks?

Religion or Philosophy

The fundamentalists' assertion that secular humanism is a religion has its tenuous legal basis in a 1961 U.S. Supreme Court decision in which Justice Hugo L. Black identified several religions that he said were not based on a belief in God—Buddhism, Taoism, Ethical Culture, Secular Humanism, and others. However, Justice Black did not elaborate on his use of the term religion, nor did he profess to be an expert on religious or philosophical systems.

Not only have the fundamentalists been unable to explain why secular humanism is a religion, they can't even define the evil doctrine. In 1984, the U.S. Senate passed an educational funding bill, called the Hatch Amendment after Utah's right-wing senator, that prohibited expenditures for teaching secular humanism. But when Senator Hatch was incapable of defining the pernicious threat to school children, his amendment was quietly dropped.

Yet, in the minds of the fundamentalists, secular humanism is synonymous with everything they despise and fear: evolution, sex education, values clarification, situational ethics, social welfare programs, moral relativism, critical thinking, and so on. An attorney for the Alabama defendants accurately described the plaintiffs as biblical literalists who use the term secular humanism as a convenient label to attack anything with which they disagree.

But the radical fundamentalists in Alabama carried their argument one step further. They reasoned (erroneously) that exclusion of the Christian religion from the schools is tantamount to establishment of the "religion of secularism." Not surprisingly, an *Arkansas Democrat* editorial expounding upon the Alabama case committed the same logical fallacy.

Just because theistic doctrines are not taught in the schools does not justify the *Democrat* editorialist's inference that atheism is therefore being promoted *as a creed*. The absence of explicitly religious instructional material is not equivalent to an endorsement of secular humanism. It is difficult to understand how anyone could reason that exclusion of religious dogma is equivalent to sanctioning "Godless belief," unless algebra, chemistry, foreign languages, and other courses are viewed as inculcating atheism.

A proponent of this fallacious argument, in a letter to the *Arkansas Gazette*, revealed the fundamentalist motivation underlying this illogic. Commenting on the Alabama case, Eddie Garrett explained that "Evolutionary secularism is a particularly dangerous kind of religion, since it removes the fear of God from humans, and allows mankind's evil nature to express itself unhindered in some men who become fully devoted to it."

The crowning testimony in the Alabama trial was given by David Hunter, a sociology professor at the University of Virginia. Under direct examination, the learned professor testified that humanism is *a functional equivalent of religion*, because humanism has a wide range of religious institutions, such a churches, credentialed ministers, Sunday services, rituals (*e.g.*, weddings and memorial services), and a service ministry. Professor Hunter concluded that humanism is no less religious than quasi-religions like transcendental meditation and est or Eastern religions such as Buddhism and Confucianism.

Under cross-examination, the professor conceded that the the First Amendment does not contain the phrase "functional equivalent of religion," but then he stated that this phrase was essentially synonymous with religion. He subsequently admitted, in a highly amusing and (for him) embarrassing series of questions and answers, that radical leftist political ideologies, modern science, bureaucracy, technology, individualism, vegetarianism, socialism, and the environmental movement are all functional equivalents of religion!

Obviously, if the professor's views were accepted at face value, no coherent secular theories or non-ecclesiastical systems of thought could pass the First Amendment screen. But Professor Hunter's basic error was his failure to distinguish between the tens of millions of *religious* humanists in America, including many Unitarians, Jews, Catholics, Methodists, Baptists, etc., and the tens of thousands of *secular* humanists, who reject all supernatural beliefs and explanations, have no creed or dogma, and don't engage in any prayers or other rituals.

Atheistic Textbooks

At the request of the plaintiffs in Alabama, Professor Paul Vitz of New York University examined a sample of textbooks approved by the state board of education for evidence of censorship of religion. The highly political nature of Professor Vitz's conception of religion was revealed under cross-examination. For example, omission of any discussion of the California tax revolt (Howard Jarvis's Proposition 13) was cited as an instance of anti-religious bias, as was failure to mention ultra-conservative ERA opponents Phyllis Schlafly and Jean Kirkpatrick.

Professor Vitz also admitted that he has been an outspoken advocate of the use of vouchers or tuition tax credits so students can go to religious schools of their own choice rather than public schools. Professor Vitz's conclusion that religion is "overwhelmingly left out" of the social studies and history texts in Alabama would be of doubtful validity if research by two reputable organizations had not made similar determinations.

After studying 31 representative junior and senior high school textbooks, a task force sponsored by People for the American Way found that "religion is simply not treated as a significant element in American life." An independent investigation commissioned by Americans United for Separation of Church and State reached much the same conclusion. The PAW report called for "a balanced and sensitive treatment of religion in American life."

Supporting the fundamentalists' complaints, Secretary of Education William Bennett asserted that it is preposterous to write about the civil rights movement of the 1960s without making reference to Rev. Martin Luther King's status as a clergyman or showing how the movement was grounded in the churches.

Secular humanists agree completely with this sentiment and endorse all efforts to accurately portray religiously-inspired accomplishments in U.S. history. For example, the monumental commitment of the Salvation Army to helping poor and homeless Americans should receive extended treatment in school texts. Similar attention should be given to the numerous religious orders and service organizations composed of laypersons, such as

Catholic Charities and Heifer Project International. The American Catholic bishops' recent pastoral letters demanding economic justice for all Americans and condemning expenditures on nuclear weapons illustrate religious responsibility at its very best.

But a balanced review of religion in U.S. history requires that both sides of the story be told. Secretary Bennett failed to mention in his example that the vicious racism that Dr. King confronted was religiously motivated. The Ku Klux Klan and other groups that advocate racial and ethnic hatred, such as Posse Comitatus, Aryan Nations, The Order, and Church of Jesus Christ Christian, which compose the "Christian Identity" movement, base their racist beliefs, anti-Semitism, and anti-Catholicism on a fundamentalist rendering of the Bible.

In fact, religious intolerance is a tradition that can be traced back to the founding of the American colonies. The majority of the colonies had established religions that were supported by public taxes. For example, the established church in New York was the Dutch Reformed Church, in Georgia it was the Anglican Church, and in Connecticut the Congregational Church enjoyed official recognition. Strict enforcement of the establishment in Connecticut resulted in whipping, jailing, and banishment for Quakers, Baptists, and other heretics.

Maryland's colonial assembly adopted in 1649 what was known as the Toleration Act, which provided religious freedom for all persons professing belief in the divinity of Jesus Christ, including

99

Catholics. Those who dissented might be punished with confiscation of property or death. Puritan zealots subsequently seized control of the government, repudiated the Act of Toleration, and executed at least four catholics. This is the kind of religious "toleration" that U.S. presidential aspirant Rev. Pat Robertson and other fundamentalist politicians could heartily endorse!

Most Americans have a general knowledge of the notorious witch trials that resulted in the hanging of 19 women and men in Salem, Massachusetts in 1692. But few persons know that four Quakers were hanged publicly in Boston in 1658 by Puritan authorities, after repeated banishments and beatings had failed to keep them away from the Bay Colony. Nor do many students learn in school about the anti-Catholic riots that occurred in 1844 in Philadelphia, when a Protestant mob burned several Catholic churches and 14 residents died in the ensuing armed brawl.

Yes, let's teach about the role of religion in American history in our public schools, because future citizens need to understand the dangers of authoritarian fundamentalism, as well as to appreciate the humanitarian achievements of people inspired by religious faith. It is frightening to contemplate what the school curriculum would look like it the misnamed National Association of Christian Educators ever attains its goal of eliminating secular humanism from the schools and having texts adopted that promote only fundamentalist themes.

Radical Fundamentalism

As everyone expected, Judge Hand ruled that the 45 textbooks challenged by the plaintiffs did promote "the religion of secular humanism." Because this violates the U.S. Constitution's prohibition against establishment of religion, Judge Hand summarily banned the 45 texts from further use in Alabama classrooms.

Reaction to this act of judicial censorship was virtually unanimous, with civil libertarians and most conservative politicians and commentators highly critical of Judge Hand's decision. Even U.S. Attorney General Edwin Meese III expressed serious reservations about the judge's ruling. Only reactionary propagandists like James Kilpatrick, Joe Sobran and the *Arkansas Democrat* editorialists applauded the decision.

On August 26, 1987, only two days after the court of appeals reversed Judge Hull in the Tennessee case, the U.S. Court of Appeals for the Eleventh Circuit reversed Judge Hand. The plaintiffs apparently saw the *hand*writing on the wall and decided wisely not to appeal the circuit court's decision to the U.S. Supreme Court. The judicial setbacks, however, will not stop the radical fundamentalists from seeking to inflict their unchristian dogma on all Americans.

Part III

Fundamentalism

and Death

Introduction

Christian fundamentalists are preoccupied with death. In fact, Christian theology is predicated on human anxiety experienced with contemplation of personal annihilation. As Rev. Billy Graham reminds us almost daily, to be a Christian means to accept the proposition that Jesus died on the cross so that believers can achieve everlasting life. That is to say, Jesus' faithful followers should not have to worry continuously about destruction of self. But they do.

Writing in support of the U.S. Supreme Court's reaffirmation of the death penalty in Spring, 1987, in spite of overwhelming evidence that it is unfairly administered, Milton Jones of Fayetteville cited Genesis 9:6. "Whoever sheds man's blood, by man his blood shall be shed; for in the image of God, He made man." In an earlier defense of hunting, Mr. Jones argued that the Bible does not teach that it is morally wrong to hunt or otherwise kill animals. The implication, of course, is that killing nonhuman animals for "sport" is also approved by God.

Illustrating a much different religious perspective, Governor Toney Anaya commuted the sentences of New Mexico's five death row inmates in November, 1986, shortly before he left office. He called for abolition of the death penalty because "it is inhumane, immoral, anti-God and incompatible with an enlightened society." Governor Anaya has opposed capital punishment throughout his political career, explaining that his moral beliefs derive from his Roman Catholic upbringing. The U.S. Catholic bishops have consistently opposed the death penalty.

The three chapters in Part III address two highly controversial issues that are basically manifestations of death anxiety, capital punishment and gun control. Fundamentalists are uncompromising advocates of the death penalty, as outlined in Chapter 13, **Jesus and Capital Punishment**. In Chapter 14, **Which Crimes Warrant the Death Penalty?**, the dogma of biblical literalism is confronted directly by listing the various "crimes" for which Mosaic law prescribes the death penalty. In Chapter 15, **America's Most Dangerous Religion**, the terrible gun problem in the U.S. is explained in religious terms.

Chapter 13

Jesus and Capital Punishment

Twenty thousand murders are committed in the U.S. each year, the highest homicide rate in the civilized world. Polls show that 75% of adult Americans favor the death penalty for premeditated murder. At the same time 75% of Americans identify themselves as Christians. It can be readily concluded that at least two-thirds of Christians in the U.S. approve of the death penalty. Is there a theological contradiction contained in this conclusion? Specifically, can a person be a Christian and also advocate capital punishment?

Among fundamentalists, endorsement of the death penalty ranks with school prayer, creationism, militarism, and opposition to abortion ("pro-life") as central issues in their political agenda. Fundamentalist spokespersons have advocated capital punishment for homosexuals, adulterers, pedophiles, and drug pushers, as well as murderers and rapists. Religious fundamentalists in other nations are equally harsh. For example, drug traffickers are executed in Malaysia, adulterers are beheaded in Iran, and corrupt government officials and businessmen are routinely hanged in Iraq.

Two Views of Life

In an article titled "Capital Punishment—A Christian Dilemma" published in the May-June, 1986 issue of *Twentieth Century Watch* magazine, Rev. Ronald Dart advocated public hanging as appropriate punishment for capital crimes. The verses supporting Rev. Dart's position were taken almost entirely from the Old Testament, *i.e.*, Exodus, Leviticus, Isaiah, and Jeremiah. Nowhere in the article was Jesus mentioned nor was any reference made to His ethical teachings as they are presented in the Gospel.

Surprisingly, Rev. Dart did not specify those crimes that he believes warrant public hanging. Considering his fondness for the Old Testament, would Rev. Dart include among capital offenses murder, kidnapping, and striking one's parents? Adultery, homosexuality, and cursing God? Nonvirginity, sorcery, and working on the Sabbath? All of these and several other so-called crimes are punishable by either stoning to death or burning alive according to Mosaic law.

The term "Christian" means simply a follower of Jesus of Nazareth, who is called Christ or the Messiah. Jesus prefaced the Sermon on the Mount by saying that He came not to replace the teachings of Moses and Prophets, but rather to strengthen them (Matthew 5:17). It is patently clear, however, that Jesus was referring mainly to the Ten Commandments, because He disaffirmed much of Mosaic law on numerous occasions, beginning in the Sermon on the Mount.

In very brief summary form, Jesus' ethical teachings that are directly relevant to the question of capital punishment include the commandments that we forgive others for their offenses against us, that we never resort to violence against others, and that we leave the judgment of others to God. For guidance, we simply have to look to Jesus' personal examples.

When the Pharisees brought the woman taken in adultery to Jesus and asked Him what the appropriate penalty should be, Jesus said "Let the person without sin cast the first stone" (John 8:7); then He forgave her. When the mob came to arrest Jesus at Gethsemane, He reminded His followers that "Those who take up the sword shall perish by the sword" (Matthew 26:52). Finally, when Jesus was suffering a painful death at Golgotha, He asked forgiveness for His executioners: "Father, forgive them for they know not what they do" (Luke 23:34).

Some Christians do not regard Jesus' teachings to be realistic guidelines for everyday living, claiming that His rules of behavior could apply only in a perfect society. To illustrate this contention, they erroneously assert that Jesus opposed all punishment. This is not true, of course, because Jesus believed in everlasting punishment as the consequence of refusal to heed God's Word. Interestingly, Bertrand Russell considered this belief to be the most serious defect in Jesus' moral character.

One conclusion with which everybody agrees is that some perpetrators deserve the most severe punishment that can be administered without violating the Constitutional prohibition against cruel and unusual punishment. The abduction, rape, and murder (by cutting her throat) of a young Dumas, Arkansas schoolteacher in 1985 by 3 teenaged boys provides a particularly heinous example. The boys were convicted and sentenced to life without parole, 60 years, and life in prison. Overwhelming statistical evidence indicates that if the youths had been black and the victim white, rather than vice versa, the probability is very high that they would have received the death penalty.

The last execution in Arkansas occurred more than 20 years ago. Governor Bill Clinton has reassured his skeptical critics repeatedly that he will preside over an execution as soon as possible. So far he has been thwarted by a seemingly endless appeals process. Governor Clinton has also stated on many occasions that his Christian faith is very important to him. Yet he is so anxious to discard his liberal image that he might just strangle convicted murderer John Edward Swindler with his bare hands if given the opportunity.

In contrast to Arkansas' unblemished record, Texas leads the nation with 25 executions since 1982. However, it is doubtful that the death penalty has been applied fairly in Texas during the past four years. In July, 1986, Randy Woolls was executed by lethal injection for beating, slashing, and burning to death a mother of four children. At the same time, Wesley Miller was turned down in his third application for parole since 1984. In 1982, Miller was convicted of the brutal stabbing (38 times) murder of a high school cheerleader who rebuffed his romantic advances. Such extreme disparities violate all sense of proportionality and encourage disrespect for the judicial process.

For those persons who do not find in Jesus' teachings sufficient basis for opposing the death penalty, three additional lines of reasoning may be invoked: logical, psychological, and moral arguments.

The logical argument against capital punishment involves a straightforward contradiction. We consider abhorrent the intentional, willful, premeditated, and sometimes gruesome murder of another human being. Then after justly convicting the murderer, we set an an example for other potential murderers by intentionally, willfully, and with premeditation, killing the murderer. Are these two acts equivalent? Advocates of capital punishment argue that one victim was innocent and the other forfeited the privilege of living. Opponents say simply that all killing is wrong.

The psychological argument against the death penalty is premised on the well-documented conclusion that the U.S. is a death denying society. Americans are typically unable to accept the fact of death with equanimity, preferring instead the myth of survival of the human personality beyond bodily disintegration. We project our fear of death onto others, believing the death penalty to be the ultimate punishment. However, because everybody dies sooner or later, execution only shortens life. A moment's reflection reveals that the most severe punishment that our society can inflict on wrong-doers is permanent loss of liberty, *i.e.*, life in prison without parole.

The moral argument against capital punishment derives from the unarguable assertion that no judicial system is perfect. Even in the U.S. with our presumption of innocence and requirement of evidence "beyond any reasonable doubt" to sustain conviction, errors still occur. Two researchers identified 343 cases of persons convicted of capital offenses in the U.S. between 1900 and 1985 who were, in fact, innocent. Twenty-five of these innocent people were executed. Because capital punishment is irreversible, there is no mechanism for correcting judicial errors.

If it were carried out regularly and without exception, would the death penalty serve as a deterrent to murder and other capital crimes? This is an extremely difficult question to address via standard social science research strategies. Still, an economist named Isaac Ehrlich concluded that each execution may save 8 murder victims through its deterrent effect. Most experts doubt the validity of Ehrlich's analyses. Everyone agrees, however, that executions are highly cost-effective relative to lengthy incarceration and that executions permanently protect society from dangerous criminals.

Assuming that it could be demonstrated to everyone's satisfaction that each execution would prevent 8 (or say 25, or even 50) murders, would such a deterrent effect offset the moral argument against the death penalty? Or the Christian objection? How many innocent lives would have to be saved through execution to justify the infrequent killing by society of a wrongfully convicted person? Can any ratio, no matter how favorable, of innocent victims saved from murder to unjustly convicted persons executed placate a Christian opponent of capital punishment?

Should Christians stand with Jesus on moral issues, or should they succumb to the primitive appeal of Mosaic law? It is obvious that Jesus' ethical teachings are incompatible with the death penalty. As Rev. John S. Workman put it, endorsement of capital punishment means literally that Christians have given up on God. Conversely, opposition to the death penalty is a commitment to the ultimate value of all human life. Contrary to Rev. Dart's thesis, there is no dilemma about capital punishment for Christians or for any civilized people. Deliberate killing is never justified and it is always morally wrong.

Chapter 14

Which Crimes Warrant the Death Penalty?

It is axiomatic among fundamentalist Christians that the Bible is the inerrant Word of God. Fundamentalists adhere to the dogma of biblical infallibility despite hundreds of inconsistencies, contradictions, and outright errors that are found in Scripture.

The doctrine of biblical literalism holds that every statement in the Bible represents divinely revealed Truth. This extreme view is rejected by the vast majority of Christians, who recognize the necessity of using common sense in interpreting Scripture.

Persons of literalist persuasion cite 2 Timothy 3:16 to support their position. In this verse, Paul explained to Timothy that the entire Bible was written under divine inspiration from God. Apparently, the blatant circularity of using a scriptural statement to document the infallibility of Scripture is no problem for literalists.

Christian fundamentalists find general warrant for capital punishment in the Mosaic injunction of "an eye for an eye, a tooth for a tooth, and a life for a life." However, Mosaic law prescribes death as an appropriate punishment for many crimes other than murder. The following types of misbehavior are punishable by either stoning to death or burning alive:

1. Premeditated killing of another person (Exodus 21:12-14; Leviticus 24:17).

2. Accidentally causing the death of a pregnant woman during a fight (Exodus 21:23).

3. Sacrificing a child as a burnt offering to Molech (Leviticus 20:1-2; Deuteronomy 18:10); sacrificing to any god other than Jehovah (Exodus 22:20).

4. Owning a dangerous animal that kills another person (Exodus 21:29).

5. Kidnapping another person (Exodus 21:15; Deuteronomy 24:7).

6. Striking one's father or mother (Exodus 21:15) or cursing one's father or mother (Exodus 21:17; Leviticus 20:9).

7. Cursing God (Leviticus 24:11-16; 23); worshipping other gods (Deuteronomy 13:6-10; 17:2-5).

8. Committing adultery (Leviticus 20:10-12; Deuteronomy 22:22).

9. Engaging in homosexual acts (Leviticus 20:13).

10. Engaging in sexual relations with animals (Exodus 22:19; Leviticus 20:15-16).

11. Having sexual intercourse with a woman and with her mother (Leviticus 20:14).

12, Becoming a prostitute if the daughter of a priest (Leviticus 21:9).

13. Nonvirginity at marriage for women (Deuteronomy 22:20-21).

14. Incorrigible rebelliousness and drunkenness by male youth (Deuteronomy 21:18-21).

15. Practicing sorcery, witchcraft, or wizardry (Exodus 22:18; Leviticus 20:27).

16. Working on the Sabbath (Exodus 35:2) or gathering wood on the Sabbath (Numbers 15:32-36).

While many of these so-called crimes are repugnant or abhorrent to decent people, others are simply unappealing or just annoying. Only a few could reasonably justify the death penalty.

Yet, it was less than three hundred years ago that two dozen alleged witches were hanged or burned by sincere religious people in Salem, Massachusetts. And it was only in 1980 that U.S. Senator Jeremiah

Denton proposed a federal law requiring the death penalty for adultery.

Although there is no doubt that some biblical literalists endorse capital punishment for homosexuals and prostitutes, surely no Christians actually advocate the death penalty for rebelliousness, nonvirginity, or working on the Sabbath.

Chapter 15

America's Most Dangerous Religion

Contrary to what fundamentalist Christians are fond of saying, secular humanism is *not* America's most dangerous religion. And despite their unsavory reputations, none of the following qualify as *the* most dangerous religion in America either: Hare Krishna, Ku Klux Klan, The Order, Black Muslims, White People's Christian Party, Church of Satan, Moonies, Posse Comitatus, or Church of Jesus Christ Christian.

What many of these groups have in common, however, is a single-minded commitment to a religiously-inspired cause, intense dislike or outright hatred of people they disagree with, and a willingness to resort to violence to achieve their goals. Broadly defined, a religion is a a system of beliefs strongly held by faith that establishes a basis for defining meaning and purpose in life.

Most people don't realize that organizations like the National Rifle Association, Second Amendment Foundation, Gun Owners of America, Citizens Committee for the Right to Keep and Bear Arms, and the Firearms Coalition constitute a form of religious expression, but they do, in fact, possess the essential characteristics of a religious belief system. Their members regard certain objects as sacred (guns), they engage in holy rituals (hunting), they subscribe to an infallible dogma (the Second Amendment to the U.S. Constitution), they look to a priesthood for doctrinal guidance (national headquarters in Washington, D.C.), and they organize themselves into local congregations (gun clubs and hunting lodges).

The thesis of this chapter is that the basic motive that results in traditional forms of religious activity, *i.e.*, the human need to manage existential anxiety, is the very same drive that underlies and sustains the gun lobby and all of its manifestations in America. A fairly straightforward case can be made to support the contention that adulation of guns and other destructive devices serves a religious function in the human psyche. It is even easier to document the dangerousness of this form of religious behavior. Furthermore, all of human history, and especially contemporary events throughout the world, demonstrates the inextricable connection between religion and violence.

There are at least 200 million guns owned by private citizens in the U.S. Despite the existence of gun registration laws in most states, with few exceptions, guns are readily available to any person who desires one. There is no limit to the type of gun that can be obtained, *e.g.*, pistols, rifles, machine guns, and anti-tank guns. No wonder that some 12,000 homicides result from gunshot each year in the U.S., a per capita rate 100 times higher than in other civilized countries. One thousand Americans die of accidental gun wounds every year and more than one half million crimes are committed using guns each year.

American citizens recognize the scope and cause of these terrible, frightening statistics; two thirds of adults in the U.S. favor stricter gun control laws. But the organizations listed above spend $20 million a year lobbying against any and all forms of gun control. The N.R.A. alone has an annual budget of $70 million! By comparison $50 million is contributed to the Billy Graham Worldwide Crusade each year.

What motivates a relatively small segment (3 to 5 million adherents) of the American population to behave so irrationally? What is the psychological basis for extreme gun advocacy? Numerous observations suggest a religious basis for the gun problem. For example, extremist religious groups like the Ku Klux Klan, White People's Christian Party, Church of Jesus Christ Christian, and Covenant, Sword, and Arm of the Lord are in reality para-military organizations that maintain substantial arsenals of guns and ammunition in preparation for a final battle with their Satanically-inspired enemies.

With few exceptions, Christian fundamentalists oppose all types of gun control and favor capital punishment for many serious crimes. Offhand remarks by religious leaders are also revealing, such as Rev. Jimmy Swaggart's proposed solution to the drug problem: put the drug pusher against a wall and use a .30–.30 on him (or her). These and other similarities between fundamentalist religious zealots and the gun lobby do not, of course, demonstrate that the N.R.A. and other groups are religious organizations. But the consistent pattern of common concerns and shared values is clearly more than coincidence.

The genesis of the religious sentiment is located in the individual's inability to resolve rationally the existential question, *i.e.*, Where does personhood originate? What is the cosmic meaning of life? What is the ultimate fate of the individual? The simple biological fact is that human personality and the experienced self cease to exist at the moment of bodily death. Nothing survives death, not the personality, self, spirit, soul, or anything else. The anxiety and terror associated with recognition of this reality can be so overwhelming and incapacitating that life itself may be threatened unless measures are taken to defend oneself. Two major strategies for defense of self are observed, one conscious and the other unconscious.

The conscious strategy is exemplified in standard religious commitment and ritual. The individual who becomes a Christian, for example, denies the inevitability of personal destruction by embracing the myth of redemption to everlasting life through survival of the "soul" by confession and atonement for sins and by "grace" of the Savior. It is doubtful that most Christians actually believe this postulate, but socially reinforcing and solidifying activities such as group worship, prayer, hymn singing, and other types of spiritual encouragement help believers suppress the potentially devastating effects of existential anxiety.

Unconsciously motivated behavior serves an essential role in the psychological economy of human beings, but the individual is never aware of the true function of the behavior. The unconscious strategy for dealing with existential anxiety is obviously not recognized as such by gun enthusiasts, because if they understood their motive, the defense mechanism would cease to serve its protective function.

Guns are holy objects for gun adherents because guns are the symbolic representation of death, guns may actually serve as instruments of death, and they thus give the gun owner a sense of power over death. Gun owners confront and manage unconsciously experienced anxiety about personal destruction by playing with death and by actually terminating life in socially acceptable ways.

The evidence supporting the hypothesis of unconscious religious motivation underlying the gun problem in America is substantial. Most people have observed the behavior of gun proponents discussing and handling (*i.e.*, caressing and fondling) a new weapon. The focus of the discussion is invariably the "killing power" of the gun. A series of physiological reactions typically occur: increased heart rate, increased blood pressure, pupilary dilation, increased skin conductivity, agitation and excitement, and increased responsivity to erotic stimuli.

Another indication of the motivational dynamic of gun advocacy is observed whenever the topic of gun control is raised. Reactions precipitated in gun proponents are invariably irrational, bizarre, and extreme. For example, knives, hammers, icepicks, and screwdrivers will also have to be outlawed because people assault each other with these implements; gun control is a Communist plot; the right to carry firearms is guaranteed by the U.S. Constitution; gun registration is the first step to gun confiscation; and gun control is part of the Vatican's plan to dominate the world.

Analysis of the gun enthusiast personality reveals several dominant characteristics: suppressed anger, poor impulse control, immaturity, intense dislike of minorities, addiction to violent fantasy, delusions of persecution, defective superego, fear of self-destruction, and an obsession with death. Thought processes are fraught with logical fallacies and bizarre ideation, manifested in obsessive, delusional, or regressive behavior, or expressed in the form of fixations and fetishes.

The most serious form of pathology observed among gun advocates is the ritual of sport hunting. (Although trapping, dog fighting, and similar activities serve the same function, they occur on a smaller scale.) Hunting is defined behaviorally as killing nonhuman animals for recreational purposes. Hunters, of course, emphasize the "sporting" aspects of the activity, including tracking and outsmarting the animal; especially important is the camaraderie of the hunting camp. The central question, however, is: What can be so compelling about an activity that culminates in the wanton killing of innocent creatures?

It is clear to behavioral scientists and philosophers who have studied the matter that hunting is a religious ritual that has profound psychological implications. Hunters are able to face the fact of death by causing it, and thereby gaining symbolic power over personal annihilation. When this mechanism is explained to hunters, they become extremely upset, rejecting it as nonsense. Their vehement denial of course, only substantiates the validity of the unconscious, anxiety-reducing function of the hunting ritual.

The only reasonable approach to dealing with the horrendous gun problem in the U.S. is to recognize explicitly its entirely irrational and thoroughly emotional roots in the unconscious realm of the human psyche. In other words, no amount of statistics documenting the loss of life and severity of injuries caused by guns, nor evidence concerning the virtual impossibility of defending oneself with firearms, will have the slightest impact on the gun promoters. This obdurate resistance to facts and rational argument has been observed previously in numerous other religiously inspired movements, e.g., faith healing, astrology, UFOlogy, nudism, and creationism.

Fundamentalism and Death

When the gun problem in America is viewed as the central emotional expression of a dangerous religion, then law enforcement policies, judicial programs, and legislative strategies that have proven effective in thwarting the Ku Klux Klan, Black Muslims, and The Order can be directed against the National Rifle Association, Second Amendment Foundation, Gun Owners of America, and similar organizations.

Part IV

Fundamentalism

and Sports

Introduction

In conjunction with the evangelical Christian resurgence of the 1970's, sports became a prominent vehicle for spreading the gospel of fundamentalism to American youth. By the 1980's, sports theology had reached epidemic proportions, as evidenced by activities such as supervised Bible study for players and coaches, public testimonials and witnessing for Christ, pre-game team prayers, and invocations by clergy before athletic contests. Outstanding performances and highly emotional victories are unfailingly attributed by coaches and athletes to the Lord's blessings.

The forefather of football fundamentalism was the late Woody Hayes, long-time coach at Ohio State University. He was the prototypic Christian sports prophet, combining a stern puritanical orientation and unabashed patriotism with a keen interest in military history, to further his relentless pursuit of gridiron domination. Sadly, his career ended ignominiously when he was fired after assaulting a player on the opposing team in front of a national television audience.

A few selected incidents illustrate just how far the pathetically absurd entanglement of sports and religion has gone. Denver Broncos linebacker Jim Ryan revealed to television viewers in a post-game interview that he had prayed to intercept a pass and

Two Views of Life

was thankful "the Lord gave it to me today." While addressing the topic of steroid use by athletes, Dr. H. Patrick Stern thoughtlessly advised a well-developed youngster to tell suspicious busybodies that his steroids "come from God and not from a pill or needle." After completing his first 100-mile ultramarathon, Dan Bartell of North Little Rock disclosed that "The other runners could hear me praying out loud in the last few miles."

The epitome of sports evangelism surely occurred when Kay Yow smuggled Bibles and other religious material into the Soviet Union. At the time, Ms. Yow was the coach of the U.S. women's basketball team that was participating in the Goodwill Games in Moscow. Needless to say, U.S. athletic officials were chagrined by Ms. Yow's proud disclosure. But then, Senator John Heinz III of Pennsylvania did exactly the same thing just a few months later!

Part IV contains four chapters. **Razorback Football Theology** documents the blatant hypocrisy and obnoxious self-righteousness that permeates fundamentalist sports programs. The next two chapters, **Male Chauvinist Hogs** and **In Love and Truth** elaborate on this theme, with special emphasis on the dogmatic sexism that is inherent in Christian fundamentalism. The final chapter, **Basketball's Greatest Scorer**, recounts the career of a basketball legend who rescued a small Baptist college from financial collapse; thirty-five years later, Rio Grande is a thriving institution with an enrollment of almost 2,000 students.

Chapter 16

Razorback Football Theology

Now that the seemingly interminable college football season is finally over (for a couple of months anyway), it an opportune time to review the status of Razorback Football Theology. This is a local mutation of a nationwide epidemic known as sports evangelism, which may be defined as the infection by religious fundamentalism of collegiate athletic programs.

Typical symptoms of football fundamentalism are religious invocations preceding games, team prayers, kneeling prayers after touchdowns (brief), conspicuous church attendance, public testimonials for Jesus, and participation in the ubiquitous Fellowship of Christian Athletes. Other reliable diagnostic signs include condemnation of all alcoholic beverages, denunciation of men's magazines such as *Playboy*, and Bible recitation on coaches' television shows.

At the University of Arkansas, three athletic department officials are preeminent in the promulgation of Razorback Football Theology: Athletic Director Frank Broyles, Head Football Coach Ken Hatfield, and Sports Information Director Rick Schaeffer. A fourth operative in the Hog football theocracy is Razorback Chaplain Rev. H. D. McCarty.

The purposes of this chapter are to enumerate the basic tenets of Razorback Football Theology, to identify Gospel principles that are relevant to the central dogmas of football fundamentalism, and to outline elements of a cure for hagiographical hypocrisy in Hogland.

Water Into Wine

Consumption of firewater in Razorback Stadium is a violation of University policy. The policy is not enforced, of course, because to do so would result in the expulsion or arrest of thousands of Hog enthusiasts at every game. In fact, any attempt to vigorously implement the no-drinking rule would most certainly precipitate a full-scale riot.

So U of A authorities wisely elect to look the other way and tolerate civilized sipping and some immoderate guzzling, taking action only when serious misbehavior occurs. It was the opening of the fancy sky boxes, however, that thrust discreet boozing straight into public view. Naturally, wealthy Hog supporters who fork over $5,000 to watch three games in comfort expect to freely imbibe the beverage of their choice.

Ironically, the sky box drinking controversy probably would not have occurred at all if sanctimonious AD Broyles had not withdrawn Razorback linebacker David Bazzel from consideration for the

1985 Butkus Award, which is given annually to the nation's outstanding college linebacker. Why? Because the Award's namesake, Dick Butkus, starred in a series of truly funny TV commercials for Miller Lite beer.

At the same time, AD Broyles was drawing a handsome fee as "color commentator" on ABC's college football game of the week, which was sponsored, in part, by several breweries. Did the moralistic AD resign rather than be associated with beer companies? No, but he became a free agent at season's end when his contract was not renewed.

When Coach Hatfield nominated Porker linebacker Rickey Williams for the 1986 Butkus Award, he explained that this was appropriate because Mr. Butkus was no longer appearing in beer commercials. Hatfield gratuitously reiterated his strongly held belief that college athletes should not be associated with beer companies. Shortly thereafter, quarterback Greg Thomas was named Coors Player of the Week. He accepted the award.

Significantly, Coach Hatfield traces his spiritual rebirth to a beer drinking episode. After an all-night binge he confessed at a Fellowship of Christian Athletes meeting and subsequently dedicated his life to Jesus. Not a man inclined to understatement, Hatfield has said that former athletes advertising beer is the most damaging thing in America today.

Two Views of Life

Coach Hatfield believes that drinking beer or hooch is incompatible with being a Christian. But Jesus was a moderate wine drinker Himself and obviously endorsed the use of alcohol on festive occasions. This is why the vast majority of religious leaders and clergy, including flamboyant fundamentalist preachers like Billy Graham and Garner Ted Armstrong, take an enlightened view of social drinking. Needless to say, everyone disapproves of drunkenness, alcoholism, and DWI.

Lust in the Heart

Acting with the approval of his superiors, SID Rick Schaeffer told *Playboy* magazine that the U of U athletic department would not provide information for the magazine's annual football feature. The reason given by Schaeffer was that *Playboy* "creates lust in the hearts of men and is totally foreign to the will of God."

Who says *Playboy* is contrary to God's will? Not the Religious Alliance Against Pornography, which is composed of leaders of religious denominations representing more than 100 million Americans. Not Henry Hudson, chair of the Attorney General's Commission on Pornography. Not the hundreds of thousands of God-fearing religious people, including members of the clergy, who read *Playboy* regularly.

In point of fact, *Playboy* is a highly respected literary magazine that also publishes photographs of scantily-clad and unclad women. In 1986, for example, *Playboy* won the National Magazine Award for outstanding fiction. Numerous prominent individuals, including religious leaders and clergy, have written for or been interviewed in *Playboy*.

After some prodding by the Intellectual Freedom Committee of the Arkansas Library Association, President Thornton and Chancellor Ferritor belatedly decreed that is was against University policy to withhold information from *Playboy*. Properly chastised, AD Broyles meekly stated that his zealots would abide by U of A policy. SID Schaeffer's only comment to queries was "no comment."

The Hog's pragmatic sports scribe, Orville Henry, pointed out that the athletic department should comply with *Playboy*'s requests for information, because a fair percentage of the young men the Razorbacks hope to recruit cast eyes on the periodical. He could have added that potential Hog recruits also pore over *Sports Illustrated*'s annual swimsuit issue, which is not on the department's *Index Librorum Prohibitorum*.

The central issue in the *Playboy* fiasco was the Hog athletic hierarchy's establishment of a moral policy that derives from their interpretation of the will of God. Private schools like Texas Christian University, Southern Methodist University, Oral Roberts University, Brigham Young University, and Bob Jones University can implement so-called Christian athletic programs if they wish. But public institutions have no business applying religious tests of any type in their operations.

Two Views of Life

God and Mammon

Few themes in the Gospel are more prominent than Jesus' commandment to reject materialism. He said that desire for personal possessions stultifies spiritual development. In his most direct pronouncement on the subject, Jesus said that it is impossible to love both God and money (*i.e.*, self).

Considering Coach Hatfield's fervent faith in Christ, it was a great shock to many Hog fans when *USA Today* divulged that the Razorback's chief evangelist is one of the most highly compensated coaches in the nation. He was ranked sixth overall with a guaranteed financial package of $180,000, which derives from his base salary, housing allowance, and TV and radio shows.

Not included in the package are contracts to endorse athletic equipment (*e.g.*, Nike shoes), speaking fees, rake-offs from summer camps, and various nonmonetary benefits such as loaned automobiles and free clothing. All things considered, a conservative estimate of the Head Hog's annual income would be a quarter of a million greenbacks.

With this astronomical yearly income, Hatfield is by far the highest paid state employee. The governor, the chancellor of the U of A, and the Supreme Court justices are poverty-stricken by comparison. What justifies such a monumental mealticket at the state hog trough? Leading a football squad into mock battle against Texas? Interestingly, Coach Hatfield believes that his fat paycheck is warranted because his work is so important.

Just think how much assistance the Gospel Rescue Mission could render with a quarter of a million bucks. Meals for hungry people, shelter for homeless families, medical care for elderly citizens, visitation to incarcerated offenders, etc. Coach Hatfield did serve a public relations stint as a bell ringer for the Salvation Army at Christmastime, however.

While on the topic of big green, it was recently announced that the euphemistically named Razorback Scholarship Fund had been transferred from a private account to the athletic department's vault. The Legislative Joint Auditing Committee had repeatedly complained to U of A administrators because the Hog Slush Fund was not available for routine inspection, which state law requires.

Apparently an "accommodation" was reached wherein the Auditing Committee will be able to monitor the Slush Fund, which reportedly stashed away more than $3 million last year alone. But the names of the contributors will remain confidential.

Why is it necessary to "protect the confidentiality of the donors" (in the words of then U of A Vice President Winfred Thompson)? Are the donors embarrassed to acknowledge contributions to a Christian sports empire? Or does some of that long bread come from unchristian sources? Like, beer, cigarettes, and other drugs.

In contrast to the massively financed men's athletic enterprise at the U of A, with a bankroll that exceeds $10 million a year, the women's program barely has enough money to buy uniforms. On a Nike-string annual budget of $660,000 the Lady Razorback athletic director and coaches are among the lowest-paid at any Division I-A school.

Why can't AD Broyles share some of the Slush Fund wealth (which generated one million dollars in interest on investments in 1985) with the Hog women? All biblical literalists know the answer to this question. It is an axiom of fundamentalism that women are subservient to men, and this clearly precludes comparable status in athletics or anything else.

Not As the Hypocrites

Jesus castigated the hypocrites who make an ostentatious display of their religious beliefs, explaining that they have already received their reward, *i.e.*, public recognition and visibility here on earth. He said further that faith would be evident in our good behavior toward other people. Still, many individuals who call themselves Christians cannot resist the impulse to harass others with their pietistic pronouncements.

Witnessing for Lord Jesus does not require a pompous proclamation of faith at every opportunity. Rather, true Christian testimony evolves from personal commitment that exemplifies Jesus' ethical teachings. Apparently, the Hog theological triumvirate, under the guidance of their spiritual guru, cannot comprehend this simple Gospel truth.

The most obnoxious example of superficial self-righteousness associated with Razorback evangelism occurs at the opening of the "Ken Hatfield Show." Preacher Hatfield begins by reciting a verse or two from Scripture, usually from the Old Testament, where violent stories abound. Now and then a kernel of wisdom from the New Testament is shared, but rarely, if ever, is Jesus quoted.

Now and then Parson Hatfield varies the script. After the Texas game he thanked the Lord for the privilege of competing with (and whipping) the Longhorns. On his Orange Bowl Special show, he started by wishing Jesus a happy birthday "wherever you are"! Doesn't he know the whereabouts of Jesus? Please take note, Thursday morning Bible study leader.

Even Coach Hatfield's spouse participates in Hog Hagiology. Ms. Hatfield announced to adoring fans in Razorbackland that she and a friend get together once each week to pray for Hog gladiators who are injured or are having personal problems. Occasionally, Ms. Hatfield and the coach pray together about the Hogs' difficulties, and these heavenly entreaties may entail requests for assistance in defeating opponents.

In a TV interview conducted before the Texas-Texas A & M game, Coach Hatfield disclosed that he believes in football miracles. If Texas could have upset Texas A & M (this was the alleged miracle), then the Razorbacks would have gone to the Cotton Bowl, thus avoiding their presumably preordained mismatch with the Oklahoma juggernaut in the Orange Bowl. But the coach's prayers were partially answered when Oklahoma's star player, "The Boz" was declared ineligible for the game.

Love Thy Neighbor

Under Coach Larry Lacewell, Arkansas State University has developed an outstanding NCAA Division I-AA football program. Residents of the Northeast corner of the state are justifiably proud of the Indians as are ASU alumni throughout Arkansas. Opinion polls have consistently shown that the majority of Arkansans, including devout Razorback supporters, think that it is time to initiate an intrastate rivalry, just like those in Oklahoma, Mississippi, Texas, and numerous other states.

An annual Hog-Indian matchup in War Memorial Stadium would be good for both institutions and would satisfy football fanatics throughout Arkansas. When U of A President Thornton was president of ASU in 1983 he publicly endorsed athletic competition between the two schools. Now he sees things from higher ground, and says that football should be kept in the proper perspective.

If then ASU President Thornton thought it was such a good idea, and the populace approves of an annual show-down, then why not schedule a game? Because AD Broyles wants to hog it all for his athletic empire. In a speech to the Little Rock Chamber of Commerce, Broyles asserted that competition with ASU would destroy state-wide support for the Razorbacks.

Don't the Indians deserve the support of Arkansans? Why only the Hogs? Is this another example of a revelation from God? Broyles explained that "there are emotions in our state that could tear the Razorbacks down." In other words, if the Arkansas General Assembly mandates an ASU-U of A game, it will kill his Porker dynasty.

Broyles also raised the specter of a devastating financial crisis in the U of A athletic department. It was a performance that masterful panhandlers like Falwell and Swaggart would have admired. Broyle's ultimate threat, however, was that only with undivided state support could the Hogs "compete against those guys from Texas."

Consistent with a "scheduling philosophy" that located the weakest nonconference opponents available for sacrificial early-season home games, Broyles arranged for perennial loser Wichita State to visit Little Rock in 1987 and 1988. When WSU dropped football at the end of last season, ASU immediately volunteered to fill the vacancies in the Porker schedule.

Needless to say, ASU's offer was quickly rejected. But under mounting pressure from Hog fans and critics to stop lining up pushovers, Broyles arranged a home-and-home series with the University of Miami to replace WSU. The perceived danger of playing instate upstart ASU caused a monumental revision of Hog scheduling philosophy!

But this maneuver will not get the Indians off the Razorbacks' back. Tulsa announced that it would not renew its contract with the Hogs after 1994, because Arkansas refuses to play at Tulsa. By mutual agreement, the contract could be terminated sooner and ASU could fill the U of A's open date.

This issue will probably occupy the General Assembly for years to come. Senator Jerry Bookout of Jonesboro, a dedicated Indian backer, will spearhead the effort to catch the slippery Hogs. If it takes a legislative edict to compel the U of A football ayatollahs to schedule ASU, then so be it. But it would be easier if Broyles and Hatfield would just behave like Christians toward their Arkansas neighbor.

Beware of False Prophets

To qualify as legitimate theological doctrine, there must be a coherent set of canonical principles underlying ecclesiastical positions assumed on secular issues. A reasonable guess is that fundamentalist preacher H. D. McCarty contrives the scriptural motivation for Razorback Football Theology.

Rev. McCarty is chief pulpiteer at the University Baptist Church, a fundamentalist outpost that adjoins the U of A campus. The word "University" in the church's name and Rev. McCarty's unofficial moniker "Razorback Chaplain" are skillfully manipulated to give the impression of a connection between UBC and the U of A. There is none.

Rev. McCarty is notorious in the Fayetteville area for his unchristian views on various political and social topics. For example, he publicly defended the murderous U.S. attack on Libya. And he recently called Christmas "America's greatest act of national hypocrisy."

Members of the Jewish community in Fayetteville have for years been offended by Rev. McCarty's references to himself as the "Razorback Rabbi" and the "old Rabbi." A rabbi is an ordained teacher of the Jewish law, and Rev. McCarty does not qualify for the appellation. Interestingly, it is a basic postulate of fundamentalism that Jews cannot be saved because they don't believe that Jesus was God.

How does the high priest of the Hogs exert his unsavory influence on the Razorback football disciples? Easy. He gathers the devotees together every Thursday morning for the Razorback Coaches' Bible Study, where "Scripture and experiences are shared and applications drawn." Rev. McCarty's militaristic attitude in the name of the Savior certainly has direct application to the ritualized barbarity known as college football.

The Porker Prelate is a ready and willing defender of Razorback Football Theology, too. When the athletic department was widely criticized in the *Playboy* farce, Rev. McCarty attacked the attackers, falsely accusing them of being anti-God and opposed to spiritual values. He then advised SID Schaeffer not to cooperate with *Playboy* next year.

Since he surely knew that it is against U of A policy to withhold information, Rev. McCarty was apparently willing to counsel the SID to violate University regulations in the service of a higher ideal, fundamentalist football theology.

Stand Up for Jesus

It is obvious to most observers that the collective dogmas of Razorback Football Theology are nothing less than a perversion of authentic Christianity. The articles of faith sanctioned by the Hog evangelists are utterly inconsistent with the ethical teachings of Jesus. Maybe the coaches should devote more time to studying the Gospel.

From a legal standpoint, the basic issue concerns the establishment of an athletic religion based on the will of God. Broyles, Hatfield, and Schaeffer are promoting the sports theology of football fundamentalism at the taxpayers' expense. They are using their state-sponsored pulpit to advocate a religious conception of morality, and this is unconstitutional.

Just last year the Wisconsin attorney general ruled that pre-game prayers led by coaches at the University of Wisconsin violated both the U.S. and state constitutions. Perhaps it will be necessary for the Freedom From Religion Foundation to bring a lawsuit here in Hogland to quell religious invocations in Razorback Stadium, end Bible recitation on the Ken Hatfield Show, and terminate the Thursday morning Razorback Coaches' Bible Study.

Not only are the Razorback crusaders violating the constitutional prohibition against establishing a state religion, they are demonstrating disrespect for persons of all other religious faiths, as well as unbelievers. Coach Hatfield could quote from the *Koran*, the *Bhagavadgita*, the *Book of Mormon*, the *Divine Principle*, and other sacred texts. And he could acknowledge the birthdays of Moses, Confucius, Augustine, Mohammed, Joseph Smith, Sun Myung Moon, and other prophets.

One wonders if Catholics, Jews, Mormons, Muslims, Buddhists, and adherents of other religions are recruited by the Hogs. And what about agnostics, atheists, and humanists? Surely not. If members of nonfundamentalist cults are considered by the Razorback staff, do the prospective acolytes have to agree to conform their beliefs to the prevailing dogmas?

Like many big-league college football coaches, Hatfield has a suite of offices that surround an inner sanctum known as the "war room." The Hog war room is unique in that Jesus' name is inscribed on the play board. Devout Christians are disgusted by the invocation of the Prince of Peace on behalf of a trivial, violent pastime. Many properly consider such symbolic exploitation to be blasphemous.

What proselytizing antics can we expect next from the sports fundamentalists in Fayetteville? A proposal to substitute "Onward Christian Soldiers" for the Razorback fight song? Compulsory religious services in Razorback Stadium before home games? Glossolalia or the handling of venomous snakes on the coach's TV show?

University students and faculty can play an important role in curtailing Razorback Football Theology. A recent report by the Carnegie Foundation for the Advancement of Teaching denounced the "shocking abuses" in big-time college athletic programs that undermine academic integrity. The report recommended that the scholarly community organize to protest budgetary disparities and other forms of sports corruption. A good starting point would be to boycott games.

If "Intercollegiate athletics is not the highest priority for a university," as President Thornton claims, then why does Coach Hatfield enjoy an annual income five times larger than the typical U of A full professor's? Putting athletic personnel on the same salary scale as other U of A employees would demonstrate that the priorities are in order.

Happily, the scandalous ecclesiastical entanglement with sportsdom at the U of A might be resolved before the 1987 season without any external intervention. Remember that SID Schaeffer proclaimed earlier that cooperation with *Playboy* was against the will of God. Then the chancellor ordered the athletic department to stop applying religious tests in its operation, and AD Broyles confirmed that his ministerial staff would comply with U of A policy.

But this puts Broyles, Hatfield, and Schaeffer in the position of knowingly and intentionally violating God's will. If they are committed Christians, the Hog theologians will resign rather than play ball with *Playboy*.

This dilemma presents a real test of the Razorback fundamentalists' religious faith. The big question is: Will they Stand Up for Jesus? Broyles is a multi-millionaire so he could afford to do the right thing. But will Coach Hatfield give up a quarter of million dollars per year? Maybe an opening for a head coach will develop miraculously at ORU, BJU, BYU, or TCU.

Postscript. In August, 1987 the U of A sports information office provided preseason football data to *Playboy*. Did Schaeffer receive a *revised* revelation from God? Did Chaplain McCarty grant a special dispensation? Or maybe Christie Hefner made a contribution to the Razorback Slush Fund.

Also, the Hog leaders probably wish that they had accepted ASU's offer, because Miami barbecued the Porkers 51-7 on national TV.

Chapter 17

Male Chauvinist Hogs

It has been at least 10 years since anyone has been called a "male chauvinist pig." This was an often heard epithet during the emergence of the women's movement in the 1960's and early 1970's. Like "beatnik" and "hippie" and many other transient expressions, "male chauvinist pig" has faded out of the American lexicon.

But, a trial in the federal court in Fayetteville established a solid basis for reviving the phrase in slightly modified form. It is not even necessary to leave the swine family, merely substituting "Hog" for "pig." Testimony given in Adella Gray's sex-discrimination lawsuit against the University of Arkansas' athletic department provided abundant justification for the suggested modification of the label.

In February, 1986 Adella Gray filed a lawsuit against the U of A alleging that she was fired from her position as academic coordinator in the athletic department because head football coach Ken Hatfield wanted a man for the job. Ms. Gray was terminated on June 30, 1985 on the advice of Mr. Hatfield, after more than 3 years of service to the Razorback sports program.

Ms. Gray was hired in March, 1982 by Frank Broyles, after she had been recommended for the position by former Hog coaches Lou Holtz and Eddie Sutton. Her duties included coordinating academic tutoring for the athletes, monitoring their scholastic progress, and making sure that they remained eligible under NCAA rules.

In her lawsuit, Ms. Gray asked that she be reinstated in the position of academic coordinator with back pay, and that the U of A be ordered to stop discriminatory personnel practices. The main evidence that was presented in the trial is summarized here.

Coach Hatfield's Allegations

Hog Honcho Hatfield stated under oath that he did not recommend Ms. Gray's reappointment because he wanted "a tougher disciplinarian." Yet, two expert witnesses in the field of athletic department academic counseling testified that providing discipline for athletes is the responsibility of coaches, not academic coordinators.

Hatfield charged that Ms. Gray did not have "a good working relationship with the faculty." A dozen U of A faculty members contradicted the coach's assertion, explaining that Ms. Gray was an effective, professional representative of the athletic department. In fact, several compared Ms. Gray's performance favorably with that of her successor, Hatfield's hand-picked personal choice, Doctor Jerry

Welch, who was described as unresponsive to faculty members' queries and complaints.

As a result of poor academic counseling by Ms. Gray, the coach claimed, two athletes became academically ineligible. One of the individuals named, Kevin Wyatt of the San Diego Chargers, admitted in subsequent testimony that Ms. Gray had informed him that he was enrolled in courses that were not part of his degree program. Mr. Wyatt said that he failed to follow advice that Ms. Gray gave him on how to correct the problem.

Referring to another episode for which he blamed Ms. Gray, Coach Hatfield recalled that a professor complained to the athletic department that an athlete turned in a homework assignment that was actually done by a tutor. Several U of A athletic department tutors testified later that Ms. Gray told them never to do course work for athletes they assisted in study halls.

Perhaps the most ridiculous charge that the Pigskin Chieftain made against Ms. Gray was that she began her vacation in the summer of 1984 one day before football player Jim Kingsby received his final grades. Mr. Kingsby was struggling to maintain his academic eligibility at the time in an intellectually demanding program of study that included canoeing, racquetball, furniture refinishing, and industrial design. Coach Hatfield thought that Ms. Gray should have waited to see if Kingsby passed his courses before she left on vacation.

How could anybody fail such classes? And what could Ms. Gray have done if Mr. Kingsby had flunked one or more of these fraudulent college courses? If the coach was so worried, maybe he should have tutored Kingsby. After all, he probably took the same courses himself 20 years earlier.

Eleven former Razorback football players, including Billy Ray Smith, Greg Lasker, David Bassel, and Andy Upchurch, testified that Ms. Gray had assisted them in their studies and had encouraged them to complete their degrees. They also said that Razorback athletes respected Ms. Gray. The mothers of 6 of the players stated that they had frequent contact with Ms. Gray and that they appreciated the academic guidance she had provided their sons.

And if this testimony were not sufficient to document the insubstantiality of Coach Hatfield's allegations, under cross-examination he admitted that: (1) He had not read the University's affirmative action policy; (2) He had not given Ms. Gray a written description of her job; and (3) He had never given her a written evaluation of her job performance.

Director Broyles' Buffoonery

The star witness for the plaintiff, Adella Gray, was none other than Porker Potentate Frank Broyles. Recently returned from a memorable performance before an Arkansas House of Representatives committee, where he declared that intra-state sports competition was "socialism" and would lead inevitably to "cheating," the ex-coach continued giving his asinine answers in Fayetteville.

First, like Boss Hog Hatfield, who preceded him on the witness stand, Mr. Broyles confirmed that Ms. Gray had never received a written job evaluation. When asked by the plaintiff's attorney how employees were informed about their job performance, the arrogant athletic director quipped, "Just by the way I look at them."

Responding to a question about his familiarity with the University's affirmative action policy, Mr. Broyles stated cavalierly that he had read it "in my time," then admitted that it had "been awhile" since he did so. When asked if he had compared the credentials of two applicants (one of whom was a woman) for Ms. Gray's vacated position with the job advertisement, the Razorback Commandant said that was "not my way of doing business."

Mr. Broyles testified that he was aware of instances where Ms. Gray gave poor academic advice to athletes, but he did not reprimand or dismiss her. He said that he began receiving complaints about Ms. Gray from faculty members just a few months after she was hired, but always delegated the responsibility of informing her of the problems to the late associate AD Lon Farrell. Ms. Gray testified that Mr. Farrell had told her several times that she was doing a good job.

Not surprisingly, the University pressed into service a platoon of administrative assistants and business college instructors to testify in support of Broyles and Hatfield. One business professor described his relations with Ms. Gray as "strained"; never mind that his wife is Mr. Broyle's secretary! Other defense witnesses testified that Ms. Gray was "irritating," "unreliable," "untrustworthy," "chaotic," "inconsistent," and "inconsiderate."

Three witnesses independently described Ms. Gray as "demanding" and another said she was "too pushy." Well, how else could she keep a bunch of jocks academically eligible if she did not persistently pursue Porcine policy with supercilious instructors and paper-pushing administrative aides? It can be concluded that the defense testimony against Ms. Gray was no more than a lot of nasty name-calling.

Doctor Welch's Connection

Exactly one day after Coach Hatfield told Ms. Gray that she would not be reappointed, he called Doctor Jerry Welch and informed him of the job opening in Fayetteville. Doctor Welch is a former football teammate of Coach Hatfield, and may have been an old beer drinking buddy, too. Remember that Parson Hatfield did not swear off the suds until near the end of his career as a "student-athlete."

Because of their close relationship when they played football together under Coach Broyles, a formal job interview for Doctor Welch was deemed unnecessary. He was immediately hired at a salary half again what Ms. Gray's modest initial stipend had been. Mr. Hatfield testified that he never even saw the resumé of the woman who applied for the position! The employment of Doctor Welch illustrates perfectly how the "old *boy* network" operates in the U of A athletic department.

In his brief courtroom appearance, Doctor Welch mentioned some of the scientific disciplinary methods that he uses to bring about better academic performance in Razorback athletes. (Recall that Hatfield wanted a stronger disciplinarian.) Assigning extra study hall attendance and withholding players from practice seem like reasonable, if not commonsensical remedies, but doling out extra running requirements sounds like plain, old fashioned jockstrapology. Or does physical punishment enhance study skills?

Not only did Doctor Welch receive a much higher salary for the same job than Ms. Gray, he was provided with extensive staff support and a computer system. Furthermore, he was encouraged to attend professional meetings that Ms. Gray had not been allowed to attend, and he traveled to all out-of-town games with the football team, while she was restricted to one annual trip to Dallas. Ms. Gray was not even permitted to eat in the athletic dining hall unless she invited a faculty member to have lunch with her.

Associate AD Farrell's Memory

Lon Farrell was the U of A associate athletic director at the time of his death. He had been a dedicated employee of the Razorback athletic department for 25 years and was regarded by all who knew him as an eminently decent person. During the last 3 years of his life he suffered from severe depression, which culminated in his suicide in April, 1986.

It is truly unfortunate that Mr. Farrell's opinions became an issue in Ms. Gray's lawsuit. Believing that his views were crucial to substantiating her claim, and sensitive to Mr. Farrell's emotional condition at the time, Ms. Gray surreptitiously made audio recordings of two conversations she had with him in July, 1985. In their discussions, Mr. Farrell told her that Coach Hatfield wanted a man in the position of academic coordinator for the athletic department.

The defense strategy was to posthumously discredit Mr. Farrell's statements, arguing that he was so emotionally disturbed during the last year of his life that anything he said should be disregarded. The testimony by the psychiatrist who was treating Mr. Farrell at the time the audio recordings were made was given in a closed courtroom and the medical records are sealed, but the general nature of the psychiatrist's judgments can be reasonably assumed to support the defense.

Frank Broyles, who called Mr. Farrell the "closest professional friend I ever had in my life," testified that although Mr. Farrell remained on the job throughout his illness, other staff members assumed most of his duties, though this was done without Mr. Farrell's knowledge. There is no reason to doubt that Mr. Broyles sincerely believed that this would assist Mr. Farrell's recovery.

But, in their all-out effort to prevail over Ms. Gray, the Razorback athletic department was willing to tarnish the memory of a faithful employee. It would have been better to have risked losing the case, rather than exposing for public scrutiny the personal problems of a good man.

Judge Waters' Verdict

Judge H. Franklin Waters evaluated the merits of Adella Gray's lawsuit against the Razorback athletic department and decided the case on the basis of his interpretation of legal principles. He did not consider the factor of religious motivation in Coach Hatfield's behavior. In particular, Judge Waters did not take into account the dogmatic sexism that is inherent in football fundamentalism at the U of A.

But, it is obvious to knowledgeable observers that the Pigskin Patriarch fired Ms. Gray because she was not deferential enough to suit his fundamentalist ecclesiastical inclinations. Defense witnesses described Ms. Gray as "demanding," "persuasive," and "pushy," behavioral traits that are utterly inconsistent with Mr. Hatfield's Bible-based conception of a God-fearing woman's proper demeanor.

The scriptural basis for sexism is given by the Apostle Paul, who surely qualifies as the prototypic male chauvinist Christian. The sexist saint deduced that because Eve was made for Adam, and not vice versa, women are ordained to be under the authority of men. Furthermore, Paul asserted that Eve was responsible for sin inasmuch as she, not Adam, was fooled by Satan. For these reasons women should be quiet, humble, and submissive in the presence of men.

Despite Judge Waters' verdict (he ruled for the defense, and the case is currently on appeal), testimony offered by witnesses for both the plaintiff and the defense, considered carefully in the canonical context of fundamentalist football theology, fully warrants branding Razorback Rulers Hatfield and Broyles as Male Chauvinist Hogs.

Chapter 18

In Love and Truth

On April 20, 1987, Judge H. Franklin Waters issued his opinion concerning Adella Gray's claim of sex discrimination against the U of A athletic department. He ruled that Ms. Gray had not demonstrated by a preponderance of evidence that she was terminated because she is a woman.

It is not the purpose of this chapter to criticize Judge Waters' decision. This is the proper function of legal experts, and the case is on appeal. However, Judge Waters' opinion contains a number of interesting statements and items of information that merit wider dissemination.

Big Time Football

In putting the typically confused and sometimes laughable testimony given by Coach Hatfield and Athletic Director Broyles into a perspective from which he could evaluate its meaning, Judge Waters acknowledged explicitly the terrible truth about "big time football":

Whether that is the way that it ought
to be or not, football in major football
colleges is about as important as any-

thing that occurs there. The entire
livelihood of the football coaches and
their staff and, in fact, their very professional existence, depends upon
whether they win, appear on television, go to a bowl, satisfy their fans,
and bring home "big bucks." If they
don't win, they don't keep their job.
The fact is that the recruitment of an
outstanding 18-year-old athlete, and
his continued eligibility to play, can
literally determine the success or lack
thereof of a football coach. . . . The
court hastens to say that it is not finding, by any stretch of the imagination,
that that's the way it should be, only
that that is the way it is.

While he clearly wanted to distance himself
from the monstrosity called big time football, Judge
Waters declined an unparalleled opportunity to
condemn the disgusting tradition that poisons the
academic mission of America's major universities.
In fairness to Judge Waters, it is apparent from his
comments throughout the opinion that he views
big time college athletics with disdain, if not outright contempt.

Scholastic Corruption

It is true, as Judge Waters implied, that football is
the single most important activity at the University
of Arkansas. Just look at the massive physical facilities, the astronomical income of the head coach,

the huge contributions to the misnamed Razorback Scholarship Fund, and the groveling subservience to the almighty Hog by local legislators.

In a footnote to his statement quoted above, Judge Waters could have cited conclusions about the corrupting influence of major college athletics from the recent report by the Carnegie Foundation for the Advancement of Teaching:

> Undergraduate athletes are used as fodder for a competitive machine that pleases the alumni and corporate boosters but violates the integrity of the college and has little, if anything, to do with education. . . .
>
> The tragedy is that the cynicism that stems from the abuses in athletics infects the rest of student life, from promoting academic dishonesty to the loss of individual ideals. . . .
>
> Perhaps the time has come for faculty and students at universities engaged in big-time athletics to organize a day of protest, setting aside a time to examine how the purposes of the universities are being subverted and how integrity is lost. . . .
>
> We suggest further that presidents of universities and colleges begin to say publicly what they acknowledge pri-

vately: that big-time sports are out of control.

Fired With Love

After the well-publicized "Kingsby incident," Coach Hatfield went to Ms. Gray's home and, while sitting in her living room, told her that he had lost faith in her and that he was going to transfer the academic coordinating duties to Coach Dixon. This episode occurred on *Sunday*, July 29, 1984!

It is apparent that Mr. Hatfield knowingly disobeyed the Third Commandment, which requires believers to "Remember the Sabbath day, to keep it holy." Surely he attended church services on that fateful day, probably twice. Possibly to atone for this grievous error (Old Testament law stipulates execution for violators), Coach Hatfield returned full responsibility for the academic tutoring program to Ms. Gray on January 14, 1985.

Then on May 20, 1985, the fickle Porker Chieftain advised Ms. Gray that he would recommend that her contract not be renewed for the next year. In his official letter of termination to Ms. Gray dated May 30, 1985, Coach Hatfield explained that the position of academic coordinator required "a tougher disciplinarian."

In an unfathomable one-sentence paragraph, Mr. Hatfield wrote, "You gave your all and were yourself." Well, who else could she have been? Not a man, alas! Rev. Hatfield closed the termination notice with the incongruous expression, "In Love and Truth." In other words, you are hereby fired Adella, with love.

Ministerial Demeanor

The outcome of the trial was obviously determined by Coach Hatfield's ability to persuade Judge Waters that he terminated Ms. Gray for reasons of poor job performance, rather than because of her sex. It is apparent from his comments that Judge Waters believed everything that Mr. Hatfield said.

He never doubted the veracity or questioned the motives of Coach Hatfield (or Mr. Broyles, either), even when other witnesses flatly contradicted the head Hog's claims. Not only did Judge Waters defend Mr. Hatfield's frequent memory lapses, he repeatedly rendered sympathetic appraisals of Coach Hatfield's confused recollections of, and even his *beliefs* about, events that were alleged to have occurred.

The point here is not to question Judge Waters' integrity or to accuse him of bias or favoritism. The simple fact is that Rev. Hatfield has a knack for projecting profound sincerity, regardless of the topic under discussion. Each Fall on his television show, he skillfully intersperses Bible verses and praises to the Lord throughout his penetrating commentary on the Porkers' latest pigskin conquest.

On recruiting forays, which often take him deep into enemy territory, Coach Hatfield must convince young athletes and their parents that their future is with the Hogs. It is an entirely reasonable conjecture that Judge Waters was influenced excessively, and possibly even seriously misled, by Rev. Hatfield's ministerial mannerisms and patriarchical piety.

Judge Waters inadvertently used a sexist phrase in describing Mr. Hatfield's justification for hiring Doctor Welch to replace Ms. Gray, suggesting that he was mesmerized by the masculine mindset of Razorback sportsdom. He stated, "It appears that Hatfield had confidence in Welch and believed that he was *the man for the job* . . ."(italics added).

Surely a better word would have been "individual" or "person." Judge Waters subsequently declared that Coach Hatfield terminated Ms. Gray "because he was not comfortable with her and wanted someone else in the job." He then concluded that "Ms. Gray's sex played no part in such decision, or at least she did not meet her burden of proving that it did."

Razorback Fundamentalism

Judge Waters did not consider the evidence most relevant to Ms. Gray's allegation of sex discrimination, because the plaintiff chose not to raise the issue of Coach Hatfield's religious motivation. Specifically, there was no mention of the principles of radical Christian fundamentalism upon which Rev. Hatfield has premised the Razorback football program.

For Christians who regard the Bible as the inerrant Word of God, there can be no question about the proper relationship of women to men: total submission. It would be difficult to locate a more forceful exegesis of the the fundamentalist position on this subject than that promulgated by Jay W. Cole, Jr. in a pronouncement titled "Women Must Give Up Rights," from which the following statements are excerpted:

> Our society is among the first in history to allow its women any rights at all under the law for the land. In doing this, we have disobeyed God's word which commands that women be under obedience. . . .

> We in this century are among the first in history to witness a society where women have rights of any kind, and here we are wondering why we have more divorce, broken families, abused children, frustrated men and less love than ever before. . . .

> In short, men are expected to be the leaders, lovers, providers and authorities in their households but they are given no such distinction from women under our laws. Instead they are branded equal. . . .

> If women ever hope to have the true
> and fulfilling love of a man in their
> lifetime, they are going to have to give
> up every right that they think they
> have under man's law and take on an
> attitude of quiet humility and meek-
> ness under God's law.

During the 1986-87 year three Razorback football players became academically ineligible. Didn't Doctor Welch provide tough enough discipline? Will Coach Hatfield also lose faith in Doctor Welch? Can we anticipate Doctor Welch's imminent dismissal? Probably not, because a different standard was applied in Ms. Gray's case. Of course, if Doctor Welch is fired, it will be done truthfully, and with Christian love.

Chapter 19

Basketball's Greatest Scorer

It has been one-third of a century since Clarence "Bevo" Francis of little Rio Grande College burst upon the college basketball scene. In just two seasons of play, he established one of the most enduring legends in college basketball.

A 6'9" center, Bevo was married with a 5-month old son when he enrolled at Rio Grande in September, 1952. Located in the hill country of Southeastern Ohio, Rio Grande (pronounced *Rye-oh Grand*) had only 92 full-time students.

Bevo was first noticed in early December when the NCAA statistical service issued its first report of the season. He was leading the nation's small colleges in scoring with an average of 45.4 points through the first 11 games.

When the second NCAA report was released on January 2, Bevo had increased his average to 46.6 points per game, including 76 points against Lees College. Then on January 9, he scored 116 points against Ashland Junior College, setting an all-time single-game scoring record for college basketball players.

In mid-January Bevo broke Johnny O'Brien's single-season scoring record of 1,051 points, and Rio Grande was undefeated in 21 games. By this time Bevo had received extensive national media attention and fans were clamoring to see him perform.

When Cedarville College used stalling tactics against Bevo, an overflow crowd of more than 7,400 spectators caused a near-riot, throwing objects at the Cedarville players and storming the box office for refunds. Police restored order and Cedarville was persuaded to resume normal play in the second half.

In February, *Life* magazine published an article about Bevo, which included a captivating photograph of Bevo and all 60 of his male classmates standing at the entrance to the Rio campus. Among his many radio and TV appearances, Bevo was a guest on Ed Sullivan's "Toast of the Town" show in New York City.

Rio finished the 1952-53 basketball season with a perfect record of 39 victories and no losses. Bevo averaged 50.1 points per game and completely rewrote the college scoring recordbook. In addition to his 116 points against Ashland and 76 against Lees, Bevo scored 72 against California State (Pa.) College, 69 against Wilberforce University, and 68 against Mountain State Junior College. But his achievements were not destined to last long.

In March the NCAA decided not to approve Bevo's scoring records because 27 of the 39 games

Rio played were against junior colleges, seminaries, business schools, and armed services teams. Ironically, the NAIA elected to recognize Bevo's 48.3 average in the 12 games he played against 4-year colleges, a record that still stands.

The NCAA's action had little effect on the public's fascination with Bevo. Following a shooting exhibition at half-time of the annual East-West All-Star game in Kansas City, the Shriners presented Bevo with a trophy inscribed "Nation's All-Time High Scorer, Bevo Francis."

How does a 20-year old youth from a poor, rural background go from anonymity to national celebrity status in less than 6 months? The two primary ingredients in Bevo's rise to stardom were an excellent shooting eye and an enterprising, publicity-conscious coach.

Born in 1932 in Hammondsville, an Eastern Ohio village with 500 residents, Bevo suffered from anemia during the first 10 years of his life. He inherited the nickname "Bevo" from his father, a clay miner who was fond of a Prohibition-era near-beer of that name.

Bevo developed his basketball skills through endless practice in an old barn in which he and his friends had installed goals and lighting. They would go to the barn on Friday night and spend the entire weekend practicing and playing games with pick-up teams from surrounding villages.

Bevo attended high school at nearby Irondale for a year, but continued to play basketball for independent teams. His family then moved to Wellsville, but Bevo was ruled ineligible for 2 years because the Ohio High School Athletic Association decided that Wellsville alumni and boosters had exerted undue influence in the transfer. Finally, Bevo was allowed to compete during his senior year at Wellsville. He led the state in scoring with an average of 31 points per game and a high of 57 points against Alliance, and he was an all-Ohio selection.

Even though he received 63 scholarship offers, including some from major basketball powers, Bevo decided to go to Rio Grande with Newt Oliver, his coach at Wellsville. An alumnus of Rio, Newt had set the all-time Ohio state scoring mark with 725 points in the 1947-48 season.

Located in the small town of Rio Grande, Ohio (not Texas as many readers initially assumed), the college opened in 1876 as a Baptist training institution under the auspices of the Free Will denomination, with the mission of educating Christian teachers and pre-ministerial students.

Although Rio became nondenominational in 1950, a slowly declining enrollment and reduced support had brought the college to the edge of bankruptcy. But the arrival of Bevo and Newt reversed Rio's financial fortunes. The basketball program generated revenue for the school, and the media attention attracted new students and encouraged contributions from alumni.

While Bevo was truly a country boy, Newt embellished the rural image with various colorful incidents, such as the time Bevo had to go home and sell a hog to pay the rent. Sportswriters obliged by emphasizing Bevo's interests in hunting and fishing, seldom mentioning his scholastic pursuits. The net effect was to create a personality with whom working-class Americans could readily identify.

After the NCAA had stripped Bevo of his scoring records due to the caliber of the opposition, many experts adopted a skeptical view of Bevo's abilities. Hence, the 1953-54 season was preceded by a spate of articles in men's magazines with titles like "Is Bevo Big-League?" and "Bevo Francis: Hot-Shot or Hoax?"

To his credit, Newt elected to meet the critics head-on by assembling a legitimate schedule of 4-year schools for Bevo's second year, including a number of major colleges. Newt was not unreasonably optimistic: he predicted that Rio would win at least half its games and that Bevo would average more than 25 points per game.

After an opening win over Erie County Technical Institute in which Bevo scored 64 points, the Rio team traveled to New York City to play Adelphi College in Madison Square Garden. The target of a media blitz, Bevo was interviewed by numerous reporters and appeared on a half dozen radio and

TV sports shows, including Harry Wismer's, Bill Stern's, Jim McKay's and Mel Allen's.

Despite a newspaper strike and minimal advertising, 14,000 fans came to the Garden to watch Bevo. In a disappointing performance, Bevo was held to 32 points by a collapsing zone defense and Rio lost to Adelphi by a 76 to 83 score. The consensus opinion of sports writers was that Bevo possessed outstanding talent, but that he was an underdeveloped player.

The following night Rio lost an exciting overtime game to a strong Villanova team by a 92 to 93 score. A crowd of 8,000 in the Philadelphia Arena saw Bevo score 39 points, including the deadlocking field goal from 25 feet at the end of the regulation period. The next night Rio edged Providence College 88 to 87 at the Boston Garden for their first major triumph. Bevo scored 41 points.

A week later against Bluffton College, Bevo set an NCAA single game scoring record of 82 points in a 116 to 71 Rio victory. Next, Rio went south to defeat the University of Miami by a score of 98 to 88 behind Bevo's 48 points.

Just before Christmas, Rio played back-to-back games against two of the country's top-rated teams. After losing to ninth-ranked North Carolina State 77 to 92 with Bevo scoring 34 points, Rio upset Wake Forest 67 to 65 on a last-second shot by Bevo. Bevo hit 32 points, out-scoring Wake Forest's all-American center Dickie Hemric, who had 24.

Reasonable people decided that Bevo and his Rio teammates had successfully answered their critics. A favorable article in *Look* magazine by sports editor Tim Cohane titled "Basketball by Barnum" concluded that although Bevo's achievements were due in part to the promotional genius of Newt Oliver, Bevo could play for any college in the country.

On January 16, 1954 Bevo scored 84 points against Alliance College to break his own record. Next he hit 49 points in a 96 to 90 win over Creighton, but was held to just 26 points by Morris Harvey, although Rio still won by a 74 to 62 score.

Then on February 2, Bevo set the official all-time single game scoring mark of 113 points in a 134 to 91 victory over Hillsdale College. He connected on 38 field goals and 37 of 45 free throw attempts. Curiously, disregarding his 116 point spree against Ashland, the Hillsdale achievement also broke the Rio Grande single game record of 87 points set by Jack Duncan in 1941.

Rio Grande was subsequently invited to participate in the 32-team NAIA national championship tournament in Kansas City, and was one of the 8 seeded teams. In the opening game, a record first-night crowd of more than 10,000 watched Rio easily defeat Arizona State 90 to 74, even though Bevo scored only 28 points. Some fans were actually turned away at the gate, indicating the intense interest in Bevo.

Then in Rio's second-round game before a record crowd of 10,500 spectators, Southeastern Louisiana held Bevo to 28 points and won handily 78 to 65. However, it was revealed later that Bevo had been playing on a badly-sprained ankle that slowed him down considerably in the tournament.

Rio returned to Kansas City less than 2 weeks later to play Rockhurst College in a preliminary contest before the East-West All-Star game. But in an embarrassing conclusion, the Rio team walked off the floor with 2 minutes remaining and trailing 50 to 56, after 3 technical fouls had been called on them. Bevo scored just 22 points in a disappointing finale to his college career.

Bevo finished the season with an average of 46.5 points per game for 27 games, and set 10 other NCAA small college scoring records. Several of his scoring records are still on the books, including the 46.5 average and his 113 points against Hillsdale.

Bevo was selected to both the United Press and Associated Press all-America second teams. In the A.P. voting, Bevo actually received more first-place votes than Bob Pettit, who went on to become one of the all-time great professional players with the St. Louis Hawks. Bevo was also selected to the 10-man NAIA all-America first team.

Shortly after the basketball season ended, Bevo announced that he would probably leave college at the end of the Spring semester due to financial difficulties. One week later, the Committee on Instruction at Rio Grande recommended that Bevo be expelled for "scholarship reasons." He had failed to make-up some mid-term examinations and had cut too many classes.

Bevo's dream of playing in the N.B.A. was delayed for at least 2 years when the board of directors ruled that he would not be eligible for the draft until his class graduated. Shortly thereafter, Bevo and Newt signed a 1-year package contract to play with and coach Abe Saperstein's Boston Whirlwinds, a team that toured with the Harlem Globetrotters.

His salary of $17,000 made Bevo one of the highest paid rookies in professional basketball. Bevo and Newt stayed with the Whirlwinds for a second season. In 1956 Bevo was the third-round draft choice of the Philadelphia Warriors, but he did not ever sign a contract.

Then, after being virtually inseparable for 5 basketball seasons, Bevo and Newt split up. Bevo formed his own touring team, not unexpectedly called the Bevo Francis All-Stars. After 2 more seasons of traveling and playing 5 games a week, Bevo finally lost interest and quit.

He returned to his home in Highlandtown, Ohio and took a job as a kiln fireman at a pottery near Wellsville. But Bevo missed competitive basketball. He played in the Eastern League during the 1958-59 season, averaging 28 points per game. Then he toured the Midwest for a year with the Bevo

Francis All-Stars, playing exhibition games against the Harlem Satellites.

In 1961 Bevo attempted a comeback with the Cleveland Pipers of the now-defunct American Basketball League. At 29 years of age, he simply wasn't happy playing basketball for a living. So he returned home to Highlandtown for good, and worked at various unskilled jobs to support his family. Bevo said that he never missed playing basketball after his final fling with Cleveland.

Now 55 years old, Bevo still lives in the rural community in Eastern Ohio where he was raised. He and Jean have been married 36 years. Bevo's health is good and he is employed by Goodyear. His only formal basketball activity occurs each November when he presents the trophy to the winning team at Rio Grande's annual Bevo Francis Classic Tournament. Bevo's only real regret was that he never earned his college degree.

Bevo is the quintessential American hero, a young man from a rural background who achieved immense fame but was never affected by the attention. One of the most widely acclaimed basketball players of all time, Bevo captured the imagination of millions of basketball fans of all ages. Yet, he remained the "bashful country kid" and "poor man's all-American" that the sportswriters called him. He just loved to play the game.

Credits

"What is Secular Humanism?" was published in the *Grapevine*, April 23, 1986.

"Secular Humanist Philosophy" was published in the *Grapevine*, September 10, 1986.

"Tenets of Secular Humanism" was published in the *Northwest Arkansas Times*, March 20, 1987.

"Jesus' Ten Commandments" was published in the *Arkansas Gazette*, June 19, 1987.

"Jesus and Secular Humanism" was published in *The American Rationalist*, March-April, 1987.

"Christian Humanism" consists of five letters published in the *Northwest Arkansas Times* from December, 1985 through February, 1986 and a letter published in the *Grapevine*, April 9, 1986.

"Secular Humanism: America's Most Dangerous Religion" was published in *The Humanist*, March-April, 1982.

"Origins of Fundamentalism" was published in the *Grapevine*, October 22, 1986.

"Heresies of Fundamentalism" was published in *The American Rationalist*, May-June, 1988.

"Should Christians Drink Alcoholic Beverages." was published in the *Arkansas Democrat*, April 1, 1986.

"Why Do Innocent People Suffer?" was published in the *Arkansas Democrat*, December 6, 1986.

"Secular Humanism on Trial" was published in the *Grapevine*, February 25 and March 11, 1987.

"Jesus and Capital Punishment" was published in the *Grapevine*, December 3, 1986; a brief version was published in the *Arkansas Gazette*, May 1, 1988.

"Which Crimes Warrant the Death Penalty?" was published in the *Arkansas Democrat*, August 23, 1986.

"America's Most Dangerous Religion" was published in the *Northwest Arkansas Times*, March 19, 1986.

"Razorback Football Theology" was published in the *Grapevine*, January 14, 1987; a brief version was published in the *Arkansas Gazette*, August 31, 1987.

"Male Chauvinist Hogs" was published in the *Grapevine*, March 25, 1987.

"In Love and Truth" was published in the *Grapevine*, October 14, 1987.

"Basketball's Greatest Scorer" was published in the *Springdale News*, March 31, 1988.

About the Author

Brian Bolton (Ph.D., Wisconsin) is a Professor at the Arkansas Research and Training Center in Vocational Rehabilitation, University of Arkansas, Fayetteville. He is a Fellow of the American Psychological Association (Evaluation and Measurement and Rehabilitation Psychology) and of the Society for Personality Assessment and has received ten research project awards from the American Rehabilitation Counseling Association. He received the Burlington Northern Foundation Faculty Achievement Award for scholarly research from the University of Arkansas in 1986 and the Roger Barker Distinguished Research Award from the Division of Rehabilitation Psychology of the American Psychological Association in 1988. His edited and authored books include *Handbook of Measurement and Evaluation in Rehabilitation* (2nd ed.), *Psychology of Deafness for Rehabilitation Counselors, Psychosocial Adjustment to Disability, Rehabilitation Counseling Research* (2nd ed.), *Rehabilitation Client Assessment, Vocational Adjustment of Disabled Persons, Factor Analytic Studies: 1971-1975,* and *Test Critiques Applied Topics: Special Education and Rehabilitation.* He has contributed 28 chapters and reviews to the eighth and ninth *Mental Measurements Yearbooks,* the *Encyclopedia of Clinical Assessment,* the *Annual Review of Rehabilitation* (vols. 2 & 4), *Functional Psychological Testing, Hearing and Hearing Im-*

pairment, *Handbook of Multivariate Experimental Psychology*, *Rehabilitation Counseling: Basics and Beyond*, *Test Critiques* (vols. 1, 2, 3, 4, 5, 6, & 7), *Vocational Rehabilitation of Persons with Prolonged Psychiatric Disorders*, *Psychology for Health Science Students*, and *Rehabilitation Outcomes: Analysis and Measurement*. He has authored 100 articles in psychology and rehabilitation journals, presented 70 papers to conferences, and written 60 book reviews for psychology journals. He was previously editor of the *Rehabilitation Counseling Bulletin* and consulting editor to the University Park Press, and is currently an advisory editor to the College-Hill Press and the Test Corporation of America and serves on the editorial boards of *Rehabilitation Psychology*, *Multivariate Experimental Clinical Research*, *Computers in Human Behavior*, and *Rehabilitation Education*. He is a charter member of the Pillars Club of the Fayetteville United Fund and of the Chancellor's Circle of the University of Arkansas Annual Fund.